SIMPLE, RELATIONAL DISCIPLE MAKING

SIMPLE, RELATIONAL DISCIPLE MAKING

ANCIENT WAYS FOR MODERN TIMES

by

JERRY WILES

LEADERSHIP
BOOKS

Most Leadership Books products are available at special quantity discounts for bulk purchases for sales promotions, premiums, fund-raising and educational needs. For details visit our website at www.leadershipbooks.com

All Rights Reserved
Published by Leadership Books.
Las Vegas, Nevada & New York, NY
LeadershipBooks.com

ISBN:
978-1-951648-83-1 (Hardcover)
978-1-951648-84-8 (Paperback)
978-1-951648-85-5 (eBook)

Critical Acclaim for Simple, Relational Disciple-Making

"Jerry Wiles' book should inspire you to live a more godly life, be a faithful witness, introduce people to Christ, and equip others to do likewise. The many impactful stories and lessons are examples of how God can use ordinary followers of Jesus to become reproducing disciple makers. My hope and prayer is that the book gets into the hands of those with hungry hearts and a passion for the Kingdom of God and His righteousness."

John C. Maxwell, Bestselling author, world's most influential leadership expert

~~~

"Jerry Wiles has put together a treasure trove of stories, tools and practices that all lead to a single point—we are all meant to evangelize others and make disciples. It's just a matter of stepping into it all, and Jerry shows us how to do that."

Patrick Lencioni, best-selling business author of *The Five Dysfunctions of a Team*

~~~

"I was greatly inspired as I read my friend Jerry Wiles' new book 'Simple, Relational Disciple-Making'. The practical wisdom he shares is drenched in Scripture, built upon a lifetime of ministry, and applicable to anyone who loves Jesus and wants their life to make a difference.

May God use this to help many experience the abundant life Jesus intended for us, and to raise up many more disciple-makers."

Kevin Palau, President, Luis Palau Association

"My good friend and fellow believer from the Jesus Revolution movement of the 1970s, Dr Jerry Wiles, has created a valuable tool for Relational Disciple-Making. He takes us into the methodology of first century believers that we will benefit from."

Roy L. Peterson, Retired President/CEO American Bible Society and Wycliffe Bible Translators

"Biographical rich, biblically fresh, and historically inspiring, Jerry Wiles gives us a treasure trove of evangelistic truth with a mega dose of gospel fervor. Jerry doesn't just teach it … he lives it, and he is an inspiration and example to me as a pastor and friend. Jerry is an innovative thinker and practitioner of inviting others into a life with Jesus. Read this book now and be prepared to be convicted, convinced, and challenged to see the world outside your door with the simple truth that you are called to go and by any means available share. Reading this book could be the trimtab that changes the direction of your life."

Dr. Jerry Edmonson, Founding and Lead Pastor, The Fellowship

"Dr. Jerry Wiles has done exactly what we need now! He has distilled a lifetime of experience in disciple-making into a highly readable, practical guide for everyone who longs to fulfill their God-intended purpose in life. Sharing inspiring stories and life-changing lessons,

Jerry will re-focus your life and leadership on what matters, igniting a passion to share Christ with others and develop reproducing disciple-makers. *Simple, Relational Disciple-Making* is the kind of book you will read annually for your personal study. I recommend it as a group study for developing Kingdom-minded leaders."

Dr. Bob Page, Chief of Chaplains, Marketplace Chaplains, Chaplain, Brigadier General, USAF (retired)

"Jerry Wiles has written a powerful and persuasive book that touches on major biblical themes, including a life in relationship to Jesus Christ, the work of the Spirit in leading us, and the mission of the church and of the individual disciple in expanding the kingdom of God via transformative relationships that produce disciples who are also disciple makers. Wiles brings a lifetime of experiences around the world, seeing the work of Christ, experiencing the presence of Christ, and thinking adaptively and creatively about methods of disciple making that are grounded in Scripture, historically practiced, and empowered by an authentic spiritual formation. The application of Dr. Wiles' knowledge of orality and other oral art forms is a particularly intriguing aspect of this highly recommended work."

Dr. Robert B. Sloan, Author, Theologian, President of Houston Christian University

"Having met, fellowshipped, and prayed with hundreds of leaders in my ministry life, I know of no leader that shares his faith in Christ so naturally, regularly, and effectively with non-believers as does Jerry Wiles. He doesn't just teach it—he lives it and embodies it. That's why

Simple, Relational Disciple-Making is clearly a transformational book just waiting to guide the reader into becoming a truly fruitful, relational disciple-maker. There's a personal harvest waiting just for you and Jerry Wiles life-message will help you become a joyful gatherer."

Dr. Dick Eastman, Bestselling author, former International President of Every Home for Christ, and president of America's National Prayer Committee

～～

"Sharing your life in Christ and getting others on the journey of following Jesus does not have to be complicated. In his book, Jerry Wiles gives many of his experiences of how it has worked in his life over these past 50 years, and how anyone can be used by the Lord in these ways. Being a beneficiary of the Asbury Revival and the Jesus Movement of the early 1970s, Jerry has been on an exciting adventure of communicating the Gospel and making disciples in ways that are biblical, simple, and reproducible. He is one of many examples of how God can use anyone and everyone who is totally available to the Lord. Like he says in his book, 'God is an equal opportunity employer.' My hope is that this book will be used to capture the hearts of many others with a passion for being on mission with God in advancing His Kingdom."

Dr. Jim Garlow, former pastor, best-selling author, CEO, Well Versed

～～

"Relationships find themselves central in the Trinity, Scripture, hermeneutics (narrative sections), evangelism, discipleship, leadership development, missions (Great Commission and Great Commandment). It therefore seems only natural that the Author's preferred mode of communication also be relational. Centered in relationships, that is why *orality* plays such a vital role in *all* ministries from evangelism to Bible translation to business as mission, theological education, etc. Join Jerry Wiles as he demonstrates Kingdom expansion around the globe through oral means. This book has the potential to transform you and your ministry."

Tom Steffen, DMiss, is Professor Emeritus of Intercultural Studies, Cook School of Intercultural Studies, Biola University. Co-author of *The Return of Oral Hermeneutic* and *Character Theology* (forthcoming).

"Jerry Wiles is one of the most intentional and joyful personal evangelists that I know. I love the easy manner in which he encourages almost every person he meets to "know the Lord." His books are so clear and easily practiced that I use them enthusiastically in some of my college courses. They are like "being with Jerry in the flesh." Now that's Jesus-like, incarnational disciple making."

Ron Boehme, Author, Professor of Leadership and Intercultural Studies, Elder with Youth with a Mission

"Jerry's book is a tremendous compilation of powerful Biblical principles for being empowered as a change-maker in this world. Honoring to the Father, Son and Holy Spirit, you will learn that you also have a unique role in fulfilling Bible prophecy. There has never been a more important time for each of us to be activated or re-ignited in our

Kingdom assignments. Read, learn, act. Every one of us has a Great Story to tell."

Jodi L. Carroll MA, Chief Thought Partner, Innertwine Consulting

"This work by Jerry Wiles is sure to make plain the "how to" of sharing the great hope we have in Christ and how we can be motivated to tell everyone we met. Most of us already know we should share our faith. As Jerry says in the book "Every living thing, if it is healthy grows, changes shape, and reproduces. That is true of believers." God can use this writing in your life to illustrate the "how to" that will accompany the "why" every Christian feels. Each chapter is filled with sound Biblical principles and countless illustrations followed by the exciting results. It has been my privilege to observe this sharing on international travels with him. IT WORKS!"

Bill Houk, Business owner, financial services professional

"I've had the joy of knowing Jerry for more than 30 years. His life significantly impacted my life in the early 1990s. As a result of his influence, I have regularly shared Christ and seen hundreds respond the Gospel since then. Jerry's new book has a very significant distinguishing factor above most books on evangelism and multiplying disciples.

Every person has divine significance and purpose. Common, ordinary individuals, regardless of their education, economic status, or position in life, can appropriate God's power, be greatly used by God, and become reproducing disciple-makers. Jerry's simple writing emphasizes that this disciple reproducing lifestyle can be lived out by ANYONE, ANYWHERE at ANY TIME."

Colin Millar, President: Igniting Prayer Action, Chief Prayer Officer: Global Media Outreach, and Prayer Advocate: Global Alliance for Church Multiplication (GACX)

~~~

"I have served with Jerry for many years and know of no other leader with such a singular focus on equipping "reproducing disciple-makers" by telling stories and asking questions. In his new book, Jerry breaks down eternally significant approaches to this fundamental call into digestible portions that could very well change your life. Thank you, Jerry, for your tireless efforts to serve the Lord!"

Michael J. Mantel, PhD, President & CEO, Living Water International

~~~

"*Simple, Relational Disciple-Making* by Dr. Jerry Wiles is a truly refreshing and compelling perspective on one of Christ's fundamental commands: "… be making disciples." Without resorting to gimmicks, Dr. Wiles maintains his central focus—Christians should consistently cultivate an intimate daily worship journey with Jesus by prioritizing minute-by-minute interaction with the Holy Spirit, and by engaging in ongoing conversations with the Father. This, in my view, embodies the genuine Return on Investment (ROI) of disciple-making: it remains relational, organic, but intentional. Your journey through Dr.

Wiles' outstanding disciple-making guide will undoubtedly leave you deeply satisfied."

Rev. Dr. Byron Spradlin, President, Artists in Christian Testimony International

∾

"Disciple-Making is very different from discipleship. In this easily accessible memoir, Jerry Wiles helps us to journey through a relational tour rooted in Scripture, prayer, orality, and practice. Each chapter helps the curious learner to understand what Jesus and the Early Church did, and if they were here how might they live out their lives. If you wish to have a surprising and impactful life, practice the ancient ways for modern times."

Rev. Samuel E. Chiang
Deputy Secretary General
World Evangelical Alliance
Orality Catalyst
Lausanne Movement

Dedication

In Loving Memory of

Sheila Kay Elliott Wiles

My amazing, godly, smart, and beautiful wife of 53 years.
Sheila went to be with the Lord on July 4, 2023, after a long
battle with Alzheimer's disease.

Acknowledgment

I want to acknowledge and express my appreciation for all the great support and encouragement I have received from the team at Leadership Books. It has been a delight to work with such gifted and talented people.

I am grateful to the Lord also for the many mentors and models He has brought into my life over the years. Many of those are mentioned in the book.

Preface

Since being radically transformed during the Asbury Revival and the Jesus Movement of the early 1970s, I've been on an amazing learning journey and have discovered many valuable lessons. This book contains an account of many of those experiences and lessons. My desire is that every reader of this book will be captured by the presence and power of the Lord Jesus and gain a greater passion for sharing Him with others.

God is at work all the time, everywhere, and desires to use everyone who comes to Him based on what Christ has accomplished on the cross. Every person, who has been redeemed by the shed blood of Jesus, been born again, and has been made a new creation in Christ, has divine significance and purpose. Common, ordinary individuals, regardless of their education, economic status, or position in life, can appropriate God's power, be greatly used by God, and become reproducing disciple-makers.

Every true believer has the capacity, because of the indwelling Christ, to share their story and lead others into a relationship with the Risen Lord. Furthermore, because of God's creative and unlimited power and wisdom, everyone can equip others to become reproducing followers of Jesus. The redeeming and liberating stories and lessons in this book should inspire and foster a greater desire in the reader to know Him better and have a passion to share Him with others.

The more we are saturated in the Word of God, informed of the work of God and aware of His presence in our lives, the greater will be our capacity to share Him with others. Furthermore, we'll be better equipped to train, equip, and inspire others to become reproducing disciple-makers.

Table of Contents

INTRODUCTION 1

CHAPTER 1 – HOW TO BE FRUITFUL AND MULTIPLY YOUR KINGDOM IMPACT...............5

The necessity of abiding or remaining in Christ, trusting Him, and acting on His Word, in order to be a fruitful disciple-maker.

CHAPTER 2 – WHAT IT MEANS TO BE A REPRODUCING FOLLOWER OF JESUS. 11

A healthy relationship with God will result in growth, change and a reproducing life.

CHAPTER 3 – HOW YOUR FAITH CAN BECOME CONTAGIOUS...17

Your life in Christ is often better caught than taught, and especially powerful when God's love is demonstrated as well as proclaimed.

CHAPTER 4 – WHY TEAMWORK AND COLLABORATION ARE SO CRITICAL.....................25

Unity in the Body of Christ will result in cooperation and effective partnerships that bring people to the Lord.

CHAPTER 5 – HOW TO BE PREPARED FOR THE UNEXPECTED. 33

Sensitivity to the Holy Spirit and an alertness to your environment will enable you to recognize more witness and ministry opportunities.

CHAPTER 6 – HOW TO RECOGNIZE AND EXPERIENCE DIVINE APPOINTMENTS. 41

Praying for discernment and actively watching for opportunities are key factors to entering and participating in Gods redemptive activities.

CHAPTER 7 – WHAT IT TAKES TO ATTAIN LONG-LASTING AND GENERATIONAL IMPACT....47

An awareness of the principle of sowing, watering, and reaping will enhance your long-lasting impact for the Kingdom.

CHAPTER 8 – HOW TO BECOME A MOVEMENT MOBILIZER. 57

A realization of the value of small, simple, reproducible systems and structures is a game changer for advancing the cause of Christ.

CHAPTER 9 – HOW LITTLE THINGS CAN PRODUCE A MAJOR IMPACT AND INFLUENCE. 69

It's important to realize the power of focusing on the few to impact the many and the principle of multiplication for spreading the Gospel.

CHAPTER 10 – WHAT IS THE KINGDOM OF GOD LIKE.....................................77

Our best source for understanding the Kingdom of God is the teaching of Jesus about the mustard see, yeast, and the nature and attributes of little children.

CHAPTER 11 – HOW TO BECOME A CREATIVE GENIUS. 87

An experiential knowledge of your spiritual union with Christ can release His creative and unlimited power for strategic impact for God's divine purpose.

CHAPTER 12 – WHY IT IS IMPERATIVE TO SEE FROM GOD'S PERSPECTIVE....................97

When you are born of the Spirit, you have spiritual eyesight and have the potential to see past the seen and the temporal to the unseen and eternal.

CHAPTER 13 – WHAT IT TAKES TO LIVE A GODLY LIFE AND BE A FAITHFUL WITNESS. .105

Coming to a realization of the futility of human effort makes us candidates for the Holy Spirit to produce godly lives and enables us to be faithful witnesses.

Table of Contents

CHAPTER 14 – HOW TO BECOME AN EFFECTIVE AGENT OF TRANSFORMATION.............113
It's only when we have renewed minds and transformed lives that we can become agents of change and transformation.

CHAPTER 15 – WHY REPRODUCIBILITY IS VITAL TO ADVANCING THE GOSPEL............119
Being a faithful and fruitful follower of Jesus will result in the reproducing life of Christ in and through us and multiplying disciple-makers.

CHAPTER 16 – HOW IS DISCIPLE-MAKING DIFFERENT FROM DISCIPLESHIP.................129
It's a liberating truth to realize that disciple making is not about programs, disciplines, curriculums, or classes, but about the outworking of the indwelling Christ, and getting others on the journey of following Jesus.

CHAPTER 17 – WHY THE CONCEPTS AND PRINCIPLES OF ORALITY ARE CRUCIAL FOR COMPLETING THE GREAT COMMISSION.............137
A recognition of the timeless principles and concepts of orality (narrative methods, oral art forms, etc.) can revolutionize the way we think about communicating the Gospel and making disciples.

CHAPTER 18 – WHY IT IS SO CONSEQUENTIAL TO BE FLEXIBLE, ADAPTABLE, AND OPEN TO CHANGE............151
Being aware of the work of God around the world can inspire us and open our thinking to new, different and innovative (yet ancient) possibilities of how the Lord can work through each of us when we are available to Him.

EPILOGUE............161

CONCLUSION............173

MEET THE AUTHOR - AUTHOR PORTRAIT AND A 1-PAGE BIOGRAPHY............181

Introduction

The idea of simple, relational disciple-making could be revolutionary and transformational for many. By simple, we are not talking about simplistic. In this context, simple means understandable. Relational is about how we relate to the Lord and those around us or those we share life with. In the following chapters, we will also distinguish between the modern term 'discipleship' (which has only been around for less than 200 years), and biblical disciple-making. We'll dig deeper into what Jesus meant when He said, "Make disciples of all people groups"

Consider how these concepts and principles can revolutionize the way the Christian world thinks about communicating the Gospel and making disciples.

- What are those ancient ways that are relevant today?
- What are the most effective methods and strategies of sharing our life in Christ and making disciples that can be useful anywhere and with anyone?
- What will it take to complete our Lord's Great Commission?
- Who can participate in this grand and awesome opportunity of expanding the Kingdom of God?

These are all important questions you will find practical and straightforward answers to in the following chapters. You will be encouraged to discover that common, ordinary people can appropriate God's divine resources and live out the abundant life that the Lord talked about in John 10:10. Some may think of that abundant, victorious, and fruitful life as the super deluxe version of the Christian life. But actually, it should be the normal Christian life that is available to every follower of Jesus. Discovering and living in that reality will give you a new passion for sharing your faith and the message of new life in Christ.

This book will enable the reader to gain a better understanding of the Lord's Great Commission and the ultimate purposes of God. Which, in essence, is about living out our life in Christ, communicating the good news of Jesus to everyone, and making disciples of all nations. That is a big task, but we have a big God, and every child of His can become reproducing followers of Jesus and disciple-makers.

You will learn how to be better equipped, and to equip others to become more fruitful members of the Body of Christ. It is insightful and encouraging to have a greater awareness of how the Gospel spread throughout the entire populated world in the First Century, before the radio, television, the internet, or the printing press. Those ancient and timeless methods of spreading the Gospel are still relevant and at work today.

Of course, our best model in communicating, training, and making disciples is the Lord Jesus Himself. He asked questions, told stories, and taught parables. He created community and relationships in ways that have been reproduced by His followers for 1,500 years without books, radio, television, or the internet. After the printing press, the Church became more dependent on print-based methods and for the most part, neglected the most effective ways that people have learned and communicated from the beginning of time. And today, it is even becoming more prevalent.

In our modern world, we are blessed to have many more tools and resources for accomplishing His purposes. We will explore the significance of the tools of this present age and the tools used throughout the ages. Many church leaders will agree that today is one of the most exciting times to be alive, and we are blessed to be a part of what God is doing in this most populous world ever! With a foundation of our life in Christ and an awareness of the working of the Holy Spirit, each of us can have an impact on the world around us. The numerous accounts and real-life examples shown herein will open the eyes of the reader to the creative and innovative ways that God has used from the beginning of time God can use common people to bring about influence and life-changing impact on others.

You may be a believer who has a heart for the Lord but lacks confidence in living out and sharing your faith. You could be one who has the desire to impact others for the cause of Christ but wondering if you have what it takes. You may have had hurtful or negative religious experiences, which has caused you to be reluctant in your efforts to witness and minister to others. If any of these describe your experience, then this book is for you. The following chapters will encourage and inspire you to take action, to be that positive influence for the Kingdom of God for which God has called you.

No matter your walk of life, if you are willing to step out in faith and engage others in spiritual conversations, you will gain new awareness and greater confidence in the working of the Holy Spirit in and through your life and the lives of those around you. As you do so, you will gain greater confidence that Christ living in you is the key to victorious living and fruitful disciple-making. Furthermore, you'll learn how to become a catalyst for reproducing followers of Jesus.

The many impact stories and testimonies in this book will show you how the Lord uses ordinary people in making disciples and advancing the Kingdom of God, and doing so in ways that are biblical, understandable, and reproducible. You will identify with and be activated by how God is using people just like you in their normal, relational traffic patterns. You'll be challenged to have a greater awareness of the many opportunities for introducing others to Christ that are all around you daily but often require creative and innovative ways to produce those lasting results. You'll become more confident in discipling others in ways that will have a ripple effect and multiply your impact on the Kingdom of God exponentially. You'll begin to recognize the fact that every human contact or interaction has the potential for sharing and spreading the Gospel.

The concepts and principles of orality are the most effective ways that people have learned and communicated from the beginning of time. You will also acquire a new appreciation for the ancient methods of the early Church and the principles of orality and realize the power of simplicity and reproducibility. Through true stories and real-life examples in this book, you will be inspired to use those same timeless methods for communicating spiritual truth and nurturing others in their relationship with the Lord.

The more we are aware of what God is doing in the world today, the greater our expectancy will be for how He desires to work through each of us. The words of the song by Stuart Hamblen, "It is no secret what God can do, what He has done for others, He'll do for you,"[1] are great reminders that God is no respecter of persons and will use anyone who makes themselves available to the Lord, and willing to trust and obey Him.

---

1 Stuart Hamblen, "It's No Secret," 1950, track 12 on *Country and Western*, Columbia, 2012.

Chapter 1

How to be Fruitful and Multiply your Kingdom Impact

A HEALTHY CURIOSITY

Shortly after moving to a new location where I took on a position as an administrator with a small junior college, I got acquainted with one of our neighbors. Bill was a chemistry professor at the college and a very intellectual man. We immediately began having conversations about spiritual matters. He was raised in a Church tradition that promotes a works salvation. He had a healthy curiosity about a broad range of subjects. Bill had lots of questions about some of the supernatural events recorded in Scripture. One of the questions we discussed was how could the wise men be guided by a star to the birthplace of Jesus, as recorded in the Gospels?

Another area of interest where Bill had lots of questions was about heaven. So, I found a book about heaven at a bookstore, purchased a copy and shared it with him. Then my wife Sheila and I started hosting a Bible study in our home and invited Bill and his wife to join us. For several months, we led a Bible study that two other couples joined us for.

This bible-study period took place shortly after Sheila and I experienced a significant spiritual transformation in our own lives. We were impacted greatly by the Jesus movement of the early 1970s and became very excited and enthusiastic about sharing our faith. We had a deep hunger and thirst for Scripture and the things of God. The Lord brought many mentors and models into our lives during that season.

Important truths about the exchanged life, the indwelling of Christ, and our spiritual union with Him became topics of discussion with friends and associates. The reality of Col. 1:27, "Christ in you," and Gal. 2:20, "not I, but Christ," became experiential and very real in our lives. We had a burning passion for sharing what we were learning and experiencing with others.

That passion was contagious and significantly impacted and transformed everyone in our home Bible study group. Bill was the catalyst. When he eventually overcame his skepticism and had answers to his many questions, he embraced the gospel and began sharing with anyone and everyone who would listen. Shortly after that, his brother-in-law Randy came to Christ. His sister, who was an alcoholic, was saved and transformed. Many other family members and friends came to the Lord through Bill's witness.

People around Bill were amazed and surprised at the transformation they observed. He began receiving invitations to speak and share his testimony in local Churches. One such local Church was so impressed with Bill's spiritual depth and insight into Scripture they called him to be their pastor. He became a full-time pastor afterword. Many people came to Christ in that town, and the Church began experiencing significant growth. Bill's brother-in-law, Randy, was in business and was gifted with musical abilities. He began to have many opportunities to serve the Lord and eventually left his business and became a full-time music minister. Bill, Randy, and their families are great examples of how God can use those relational witnesses and disciple-making efforts. Up close and personal is the ideal way of communicating the Gospel and making disciples.

DISCIPLES WHO MAKE DISCIPLES

Unlike with Randy, in many cases, it's not always possible to maintain ongoing connections when we lead them to faith in Christ. In those cases, it is good to know that the Holy Spirit is creative and unlimited in the ways it can complete His work in those we introduce to Christ. Philippians 1:6 tells us, that He who has begun a good work in you will complete it until the day of Jesus Christ.

An example of not having prolonged contact with a disciple, is another businessman I had the opportunity of leading to the Lord. He began immediately sharing his testimony with his co-workers, family, and friends. He led his boss to the Lord and witnessed several of his customers. He shared the Gospel with his brother back in his home country in the Middle East over the phone. His brother later became a pastor in that country. These are great examples of how God uses His word and how one transformed life can impact so many others. Even new believers can share their testimonies and the Gospel and be instrumental in others' coming to the Lord.

Both of the above stories show how one person can ripple out to have a big impact. Over the years it has been a delight to come across people who came to the Lord through the ministry of my father, who was a pastor for more than 60 years. Some of those people are now pastors, missionaries, Church leaders, and followers of Jesus in various professions. We seldom know the multiplying impact that one transformed life can have over time. However, we know that God honors His Word and will use even our most feeble efforts to share with and bless the people around us.

THE IMPACT OF TRANSFORMED LIVES

We seldom know how God is at work in people's lives and how He has prepared the hearts of those we rub shoulders with every day until we engage them in conversation and learn something about them. However, we can have confidence that the Holy Spirit is at work at all times and in all places to draw people to Himself.

As we consistently and faithfully sow the seed of the Word of God into the lives of others, we can count on the fact that it will accomplish the purposes for which He sent it. From Scripture, we know that some sow, some water, and some reap the harvest, but it is God who gives the increase and continues His work in the hearts of those we share it with.

Sometimes we may think we are not qualified or equipped to be effective disciple makers. It is encouraging to know how the Lord uses ordinary people and ordinary circumstances to accomplish His purposes for fruitful and multiplying kingdom impact. Years ago, one of my mentors emphasized that there is no such thing as a great man or woman of God. There is only a great God, and He is willing to be as great as He is in and through anyone who is available to Him and obedient to His Word. That realization will certainly give us confidence that each of us can be fruitful and have a multiplying impact.

Finding common ground around the life, Spirit, and teachings of Jesus allows for overcoming major differences. Connecting, communicating, and listening are all vital elements in being fruitful and multiplying our impact for the sake of the Great Commission. There are significant lessons that we in the western world can learn from more relational, communal oral cultures. The global community of learning and practice continues to grow around these simple but profound, methods and strategies of orality. These concepts of orality are important and will be addressed in more detail in later chapters.

With all that is going on in the world these days, we're discovering more creative and innovative ways of spreading the gospel and making disciples. From my laptop, I frequently lead or participate in online training events, webinars, and conference calls with people from all over the world. Modern technological and media resources enable us to train, equip and mobilize massive numbers of disciple-makers everywhere. Phone conversations are also a great way of sharing the Gospel. The Lord is giving us many new opportunities to be fruitful and multiply in these modern technological yet trying times. However, still the most effectives methods are the ancient ways of personally and relationally sharing our life in Christ.

It's encouraging to realize that we, as followers of Jesus, can bloom, flourish and be fruitful. Regardless of our outward circumstances, knowing that God is working all things out after His own eternal purposes is comforting! The principle of sowing and reaping can motivate us to pursue His purposes. It is important to keep in mind that we always reap what we sow after we sow and more than we sow. His Word will not return void but will accomplish His purposes as we faithfully sow into the lives of others.

CONCLUSION

Bill and Kay, Randy and Jan, their families, and their circle of friends all found these principles to be true and experienced them in ways beyond their imaginations. That's often the way the Lord works. He is often doing immeasurably more than all we can ask or think. That makes our life in Christ and our walk with God very exciting. He is certainly willing and able to use you as you step out in faith, act on

His word, and trust Him for the results. The Word of God is living and active, and the Holy Spirit is still at work to bear witness to the truth as we share it with others.

A former pastor of mine used to say, "We should stay in the Word until the Word gets in us and gets out to others." Of course, multiple methods are now available for taking in the Word of God beyond simply reading the text. Today with all the modern technological resources, we can listen, meditate, and reflect on God's Word and experience the fact that faith comes by hearing and hearing the Word of God. It renews our minds and transforms our lives.

Chapter 2

What It Means to Be A Reproducing Follower of Jesus

IMMEDIATE WITNESS

Ashok was a Hindu university student from India. He visited a Church meeting where I met him for the first time. After the meeting, he asked me a lot of questions about religion and spiritual matters. He was interested and receptive to learning more about the Christian faith. He was especially open for my sharing with him about the life, teachings, and Spirit of Jesus.

I was able to share with Ashok about the purpose of God, the person and work of Christ, and what it means to be a follower of Jesus. The idea of being born again, as we learn about from John 3, made a lot of sense to Ashok. He was open to having prayer with me, so, as I prayed with him. The Holy Spirit seemed to convince him of his need for the Lord. We talked about what it means to confess, believe, and call on the Lord, to be saved from our sins, as recorded in Romans 10.

Sometimes new converts immediately have a desire to share their new-found faith in Christ with others. That evening when Ashok returned to his apartment, he shared his experience with his roommates and about our conversation. One was a graduate student from Pakistan named Imran. Imran was a former Muslim who had become an atheist. However, he became interested in learning about American religions, mainly Christianity.

Someone had given Imran a Bible shortly after he arrived in the United States. He read the first five books of the Old Testament and the first seven books of the New Testament. He then began looking for someone to tell him how to become a Christian. He spoke with several fellow students at the university. None were willing or able to share with him the way of salvation. He even went to a local Church to visit with a pastor. The pastor asked him about his visa status and finances but never got around to sharing the Gospel with him.

The day after my conversation and prayer with Ashok, I got a phone call from Imran. He requested we get together and talk. From there I began having a series of conversations with him. Having spent time in Pakistan years ago gave me instant rapport with Imran. After a few days of reflection and contemplation, Imran embraced the Gospel and confessed his faith in Christ. I was leading a weekly Bible study at the time, and Imran joined it. I was able to disciple him over a period of months, and he eventually joined the staff of a ministry I was serving with at the time.

Imran wrote a letter shortly after receiving Christ, including his testimony and scripture passages about salvation. He sent it to several of his family and relatives back in Pakistan. One of his cousins called him on the phone. He wanted to verify if the letter was actually from Imran. When he verified that it was, his cousin told him he would be stoned to death if he returned to Pakistan. Eventually, Imran was cut off from all his family and relatives when they learned he had embraced the Christian faith.

GROUNDED IN THE WORD

The ministry I was working with Imran with was an international Christian broadcasting and publishing organization. It produced a through-the-Bible reading guide with a devotional commentary. I had the opportunity of supervising Imran's work translating the devotional material into Urdu. In preparation for his translation work, I encouraged him to read the devotional material, as well as the related Bible passages in Urdu and several English translations. That exercise was instrumental in getting Imran well-grounded in the Scriptures.

Imran began receiving invitations to share his testimony and teach the Bible in Churches and various Bible study and prayer groups. People were amazed and surprised at his spiritual depth and insight. Interestingly, he knew very little about Christianity or Church traditions before coming to the United States. It was refreshing to observe how he simply took the message of the Bible at face value, unfiltered through any Church or religious tradition. In many ways it was an advantage for him to focus on the person and work of Jesus, rather than some religious belief system.

About the time Imran was completing the translation work of the devotional commentary from Genesis to Revelation, the Lord connected us with some other Pakistani Christian leaders. We then got the commentary published in Urdu and distributed 10,000 copies to pastors and Church leaders throughout Pakistan. We were told it was the first through-the-Bible commentary to be produced in Urdu.

Imran became a reproducing follower of Jesus. Through the witness and speaking opportunities Imran begin to have, he was able to share his message to many people. Also, the Urdu devotional commentary became a tool for equipping and encouraging pastors and church leaders throughout Pakistan in their disciple-making efforts. Imran went on to become an articulate spokesperson and an effective disciple-maker. He later attended seminary and became a missionary.

A NEW WAVE OF AWAKENING

Seasons of revival and spiritual awakening are times of defining moments, transformation, and reproducing followers of Jesus. In 1974, in San Antonio, TX, I was introduced for the first time to Major W. Ian Thomas, founder of Torchbearers International. This was during a season of renewal, revival, and transformation for many of us. The Asbury Revival and Jesus Movement were having a ripple effect around the United States and beyond. In the spring of that year, my wife Sheila and I visited friends in San Antonio in hopes of hearing Jack Taylor, pastor of Castle Hills Baptist Church and author of the best-selling book *The Key to Triumphant Living*. His book was given to me by my friend Wayne Belt and was used mightily by the Lord, significantly impacting many people's lives.

Rather than hearing Jack Taylor on that trip, Ian Thomas was the guest speaker at the Church for a series of meetings all that week. For me personally, it was through Major Thomas that I received fresh insight and understanding of the significance of Gal. 2:20 and Col. 1:27. Experiencing the realization of Christ living in me gave me a renewed passion for sharing Him with others. In subsequent years, I began seeing more people come to Christ, just accidentally, than I had before on purpose. Major Thomas' book, *The Saving Life of Christ,* **is one that** gives a great summation of what it means to have Christ living in us and communicating His life through us.

The very foundation of the Christian life is Christ Himself taking up residence in the believer, by means of the Holy Spirit. In spiritual union with Christ, we are new creations and indwelt by the very life of God. According to John chapter 15, it is clear that it is the outworking of the indwelling Christ that produces lasting fruit. These are common themes we learn from the ministries and writings of Jack Taylor and Ian Thomas. They are essential ingredients for being reproducing followers of Jesus.

CONCLUSION

Every living thing—if it is healthy—grows, changes shapes, and reproduces. That is especially true of believers, and God's Word confirms that in John's Gospel when Jesus talks about being branches of the true vine. As followers of Jesus, we bear and reproduce fruit, but God is the ultimate producer. We can count on the fact that if we are abiding or remaining in Christ, we can bear much fruit. Our being reproducing followers of Jesus depends on our being joined to the Lord, the true vine, and continually abiding in and trusting Him.

Chapter 3

How your Faith can become Contagious

BRIEF ENCOUNTERS CAN CHANGE LIVES

Many times, a so-called chance encounter can turn out to be a life transforming experience. While entering a hotel through a revolving door in downtown Nashville, TN, I met a man exiting the lobby. I smiled and greeted him as we crossed paths through the revolving doors. Immediately the man turned around and followed me back to the hotel entrance.

He approached me and asked, "Do I know you? Have we met before?"

"I don't think so, but we may have a mutual friend," I replied.

"Who would that be?" He asked.

I replied, "The Lord Jesus Christ, do you happen to know Him?"

Well, that brief encounter gave me the opportunity to engage the man in a spiritual conversation. He was familiar with the Gospel but had never personally become a follower of Jesus. He was obviously interested and open to the Lord, and we had the opportunity to share and pray together. He called on the Lord. I explained that he didn't have to be in a Church building or go through a long religious ritual to enter a relationship with Jesus. From Romans 10, we discussed what it means to confess, believe, and call on the Lord to be saved. When our relationship with the Lord is healthy and we are continually seeking to please God, we can fully expect our faith to become contagious. It should be a natural, or should I say supernatural, and spontaneous out working of the indwelling Christ.

This man is like so many people in our world today. He was a nominal Christian but had never come into a vital relationship with Christ. Churches are full of those kinds of individuals. In fact, Billy Graham said years ago that he thought that perhaps half of those who attend church in the United States every Sunday have never really been born again. That is probably true today as well.

We know from Scripture that all have sinned and come short of the glory of God. This man knew about Jesus but just needed a little encouragement to respond to the Lord. In many cases, when we witness to someone, we simply become part of a stream of other witnesses who have had some spiritual influence on their lives. It's important to keep in mind that some sow, some water, and some reap, but it is God who gives the increase. We simply have the privilege of being God instruments and messengers.

One of the big needs in the world today is for followers of Jesus to recognize that we are all ministers of reconciliation, as taught in II Corinthians 5. We are to be representatives or ambassadors of Christ. That awareness should be a motivation for each of us to be intentional and proactive in sharing the message with others.

When our deeds and our words are consistent with our message and demonstrate the love and truth of Jesus, our faith can become contagious. It's really a supernatural work of the Holy Spirit, not our human effort, that touches hearts and transforms lives.

The apostle Peter tells us to always be ready to give an answer for the hope that is in us. I exchanged a few brief comments with a lady seated next to me on a flight to Central America. I remarked that I worked with an organization called Living Water International and that we help people with clean water solutions. I went on to explain how we share the love of God and help people become followers of Jesus.

Then she asked me, "What happens when a person dies?" Well, it turned out the lady's mother had passed away that morning, and she was on her way home to help with funeral arrangements. We talked for about an hour, and I was able to minister to her distress during that time of loss and pain. In fact, we had prayer together, and she received Christ into her life.

That encounter on that flight is a good example of how we don't know what is going on in people's lives until we connect with them and listen. In the above story, the woman's heart had already been prepared and she was open to hear about spiritual matters. It is important to listen not only to people's stories and their pain but also listen and be sensitive to the Holy Spirit's direction. He will often give us an appropriate message or word of encouragement just for that person's situation. The more we connect with people and listen to their stories, the more the Holy Spirit will open those divine encounters and turn them into life-changing experiences.

THE VALUE OF STORIES AND QUESTIONS

A valuable lesson we have learned using orality methods and strategies over the years is how it connects people and builds community. Not only do the participants learn stories and discover their meaning and applications, but they also connect with other people's stories. The training also enhances relationships and builds trust among participants. Of course, the main purpose of the training is primarily for two things, sharing our faith, and making disciples. When those objectives are achieved, participants' faith will certainly become contagious.

Several years ago I led an orality training workshop with a church group of mostly senior citizens. The training helped them realize how little they really knew about each other. Even though many of them had been attending Church together for more than twenty-five years, they discovered they really didn't know one another in a deep spiritual way. They were amazingly enthusiastic to engage on a personal level and hear each other's stories and testimonies. By the middle of the afternoon of the workshop, they were in tears as they heard each other's stories, testimonies, and spiritual journeys Participants shared about the storms of life they had faced, how they had experienced God's grace and provision, how they related to the story of Nicodemus and being born again, and how God had answered prayer and intervened in their lives. The training provided a great bonding and bridgebuilding experience. A unified body will normally result in a more positive collective witness to the community.

GETTING IN ON WHAT GOD IS UP TO

One of my mentors, the late Manley Beasley, used to say that one of our biggest need is to **find out what God is up to and get in on it**. Henry Blackaby puts it another way. He says we should **identify the activity of God and join Him**. Well, we know from Scripture that God is up to reconciling the world unto Himself. He is about redeeming His creation, and He sent the Lord Jesus into the world to seek and save the lost. He now lives in us, who are born of His Spirit, to carry out that purpose. In Christ, we are new creations, we are in spiritual union with the Living God, and we are complete in Him. Therefore, there is now no condemnation (and no separation) for those who are in Christ Jesus—what a privilege we have of being co-laborers with Him in His eternal purposes.

The more these truths become a part of our lives and lived out on a consistent bases, the more our faith will become contagious. When we think of reproducing disciple makers, it's really an impartation of the life and truth of Jesus. He is the ultimate disciple maker, and He lives in us to reproduce His life in and through us.

SHORT ENCOUNTERS—ETERNAL IMPACT

There are many simple ways to connect with people in everyday situations that can change lives. As we pray for God to prepare our own hearts and give us a sensitivity to the needs of those around us, we can have confidence that the Lord will honor and answer those prayers. Another important part of the prayer aspect is simply asking people we connect with how we can pray for them. That question often leads to significant connections for witness and ministry opportunities.

It is important to be alert to our environment and be an observer of people. While at a restaurant during a slack time of the day, I had the opportunity of sharing and praying with one of the servers named Gloria. At the end of her shift, one of her co-workers approached our table. I mentioned that Gloria, her friend and co-worker, had just received Christ into her life. Then I asked her if she had come to know the Lord personally. She had not, so we were able to share and pray with her as well.

As my friend and I paid our bill, we mentioned to the checkout person that Gloria and Beverly received Christ that evening. An army trooper was behind me in line to pay his bill and overheard our conversation. I asked him if he had been born again, and his response was, "No, but I'm right on the verge." Well, that is a good clue that he had a prepared heart. Similar to how a virus can be contagious and spread to others, the good news of Jesus can be contagious and spread. The soldier in this case was impacted simply by overhearing what was said to another person.

We like to emphasize often that we all live in a mission field made up of our families, neighbors, co-workers, and friends. Those short-term connections we make daily in our normal traffic patterns can become divine appointments and life-changing opportunities. One of the things I've run into over the years is people who fear sharing their faith and introducing others to Christ. We often think of it as more complicated and complex than it really is. When we have confidence in the power of the message, it frees us to not be too concerned about our presentation or communication skills.

LESSONS FROM JESUS AND THE EARLY CHURCH

It is good to keep ourselves reminded that the lessons we learn from Jesus and the Early Church are timeless. Those simple orality-based methods were how the good news of Jesus spread throughout much of the world during the First Century. That, of course, was before radio, television, the internet, or even the printing press was invented.

Some of the new and innovative ways being promoted in modern times are just a rediscovery of the ancient ways that have been neglected. Many people are discovering the need to return to the roots of how the original Jesus movement started over 2,000 years ago. A mission leader has said that the Gospel started out like a ping pong ball; now, it's like a bowling ball. So, one of the big needs in the Church world today is to get back to the basics. These are the important questions about getting back to basics:

- What is the essence of the Gospel?
- What does it mean to be a disciple?

- What should disciples do?
- What is a Church?
- Why do Churches exist?

The answers to these questions and the discussions that they provoke can have a transformational impact on people's thinking and actions. Sometimes it's necessary to rethink, unlearn and relearn certain things to make our message and methods biblical, cross-cultural, reproducible, and transferable to everyone.

OPENNESS TO THE GOSPEL

With all the negative and discouraging things happening in the world today, God is still doing amazing work. We just need to have spiritual eyes and discernment to recognize God's redemptive activities all around us. The Lord desires for each of us to connect with Him, connect with one another and reach out to those who need Him. Some have observed that more people are open to spiritual conversations these days than there are believers actively reaching out to share the Gospel. That means there's an awesome opportunity out there today for those willing to be available to the Kingdom of God. The opportunity to make a difference, be aware, look around, and connect with those lost souls looking for what they don't know, that which can only be fulfilled by a relationship with their Creator, Jesus.

God often shows up in the darkest of places and in the most difficult times. There really are no degrees of difficulty with God. Sometimes, those who seem to be the most resistant to the things of God are more open than seemingly good people. My son and I were in a park years ago and met a very rough-looking man with many tattoos on his body. One of the tattoos on his shoulder read, "Sinner."

After engaging the man in casual conversation, I asked him, "You really do see yourself as a sinner, don't you?" He said, "Yes," That, of course, opened the door for sharing the Gospel, and he received Christ. That experience reinforced to me the fact that we should never judge according to appearance but judge righteously, as the Scriptures tell us.

CONCLUSION

Similar to how a contagious disease can spread to others, the Gospel and our life in Christ can become contagious and spread. When we trust and obey, as the famous hymn says, we can fully expect that our faith will become contagious. Knowing, believing, receiving, and acting on the truth of God are the simple steps to make that a reality.

More than forty years ago, the Lord brought to my mind Proverbs 13:20, which says, "He who walks with wise grows wise," So, I began to pray that the Lord would lead me to men and women with godly wisdom. It is amazing how the Lord answered that prayer and I was able to meet and get to know people who have been great blessings in my life and growth in the Lord. Several of the individuals the Lord brought into my life, in answer to that prayer, were notable leaders, authors, retired missionaries and other godly men and women. Praying the Word and claiming God's promises is a powerful concept in terms of our journey of sharing Christ and making disciples. Never underestimate the power of prayer. It makes all the difference in the world!

Chapter 4

How Unity in the Body of Christ can Enhance Teamwork and Collaboration

FINDING COMMON GROUND

In many cities and communities around the world churches do not cooperate or work together very well. When pastors and church leaders are willing to get together, pray together and get to know each other, the barriers come down and they find ways of joining efforts for the good of their cities. Pastors in East Africa discovered they had more in common than the things that divided them. What was the key to this important discovery? It was their participation in an orality training workshop sponsored by Living Water International.

Pastors and Church leaders are discovering many benefits of Bible storying and orality training. They are learning that telling stories, asking questions, listening, and engaging in heart-level conversations can help resolve conflict, remove barriers, and build bridges. Individual members of local congregations and communities are experiencing greater unity and connectivity by participating in the training. Participatory learning and engaging conversations are aiding in creating better teamwork and strategic collaboration that matters.

From what we learn about the life, Spirit, and teachings of Jesus, we know that oneness and unity in the Body of Christ is a command that is very important to achieve if the Church is to function effectively. The 17th chapter of the Gospel of John makes that abundantly clear. However, in a practical way, how do we achieve unity? How can the Body of Christ be unified when there is so much diversity and division among the various denominations and traditions within the Church?

Perhaps an even more important question would be, "How can any group, community, organization, or a family have unity?" Well, effective communication and trusting relationships are the most basic building blocks to oneness and unity anywhere with any group of people. From a biblical perspective, the Spirit of reconciliation (the Spirit of Jesus) is the basis for resolving conflict and division, leading to genuine unity, teamwork, and effective collaboration.

There are reports from many parts of the world where God's people are putting aside minor or secondary differences for the greater purposes of God. They find common ground for more collaboration, unity, and unified efforts to solve problems and reach the lost. This is nothing new and hopefully can be used to advance the Kingdom of God. There seem to be more questions than answers these days. There is a tendency to ask "why" questions when asking "how and what" questions might be more productive. When crises come, maybe we should ask, "how should I respond, and what can I do?" instead of "why did the crisis happen to me?"

Families have reported how Bible storying and orality training has better equipped them with tools for more effective family devotions. Simply telling and discussing the stories over mealtimes can foster greater family unity. It also equips children to communicate the Gospel. When children learn stories, they tend to tell the stories. When the stories are from the Word of God, shared in the power of the Spirit, they are guaranteed to make an eternal impact. (Isaiah 55:11)

POWER OF SMALL, SIMPLE, REPRODUCIBLE

Many church leaders and pastors would appreciate having better methods of achieving unity in their congregations. One pastor in Haiti caught the vision for using orality strategies in his Church. It resulted in greater unity and growth of his congregation, as well as more effective disciple-making. Orality strategies enabled him to better equip, train and mobilize storytelling evangelists no matter their education, gender or age. In the orality movement, many are discovering that the simple teachings of Jesus and the examples from the early Church are often overlooked in our modern Western, post-reformation Church cultures. This is what the orality movement is trying to restore.

The rapidly reproducing disciple-making and Church-planting movements are primarily in the Global South and among oral cultures. They seem to be leading the way back to the roots of the first-century Church. Their ancient methods are simple and universal in their applications. Hopefully and prayerfully, we can see an awakening in the Global North and Western World in the days ahead, much like what is happening now in other parts of the world.

The concepts of orality, or ancient methods of learning and communicating, are not a part of the thinking of many modern western mission or church leaders. However, once people observe and experience them, it changes the way the think and they gain new understanding of their application. We often emphasize that orality is better experienced than explained. As a result of the training being more engaging and participatory, it builds relationships and community. That set the stage for more effective teamwork and collaboration.

The pandemic of 2020 caused many of us to think of different and creative ways to do ministry and missions. Crisis times have often fostered new innovative and creative ways to work together. In a way the pandemic opened up some creative ways to bring church and mission leaders together through webinars and conference calls on a global level. There was a sense of unity and collaboration around some common causes.

When talking about modern technology, we like to refer to the tools of the age and the tools of the ages. Orality and oral art forms have been around from the beginning of time. Song, dance, drama, poetry, proverbs, and parables are all part of the orality domain. Of course, storytelling is universal and can cross all barriers and borders.

SHARING CHRIST BY ALL MEANS

In the 1980s, I began hearing reports of how Churches were being started and reproducing in remote areas through radio broadcasts. One program consisted of simply reading Scripture at dictation speed, with no commentary. What was discovered later was that students were copying the Scriptures, reproducing, and distributing them to others. Discussion and storytelling groups were springing up around the person of Jesus. Churches were being planted, growing, and reproducing. This is a great example of how God uses multi-model methods to spread the Gospel and advance the work of the Church. In this case, it included oral or spoken methods, modern technology, and print-based media. God often uses different individuals and groups or organizations to accomplish His purposes of spreading the Gospel.

Those in the Global Mission Movements like to emphasize how God uses all means available to communicate the Gospel and reproduce disciple-making movements. Of all the ways and means the Lord has used and is using, most people have come to faith in Christ through personal contact and orality-based methods. The rapid growth of the Kingdom these days is normally among cell groups, small, simple, organic, house Churches, and communities of Jesus' followers. Congregations can meet in homes, board rooms, storefronts, hotel conference centers, schools, under trees, and many other expressions of the Body of Christ.

Small, simple reproducible systems and structures seem to be a resounding theme in the global church and mission world in recent years. Mega churches, large institutions and organizations have their place and are an important part of God's kingdom work. However, they are not very reproducible and there is a lot of cost and maintenance required. We've also discovered that smaller congregations and organizations are more open to partnerships and collaborative relationships.

For many years Living Water International has partnered with Churches and mission organizations around the world. A significant partnership has been in Burkina Faso, where there is a fast-growing Church-planting movement. That team effort or collaborative relationship consisted of Living Water International, American missionaries and local churches. The country is a primary oral culture where Churches have no buildings but meet under trees. The pastors have no seminary training, and there was no Scripture in their language until recently. The teamwork and partnership efforts with Living Water International have accelerated the spread of the Gospel through Bible storying and orality training. Women, men, and children who have no formal education become storytelling evangelists. We in the Western world can learn from movements like these about spreading the Gospel, making disciples, and planting Churches.

FOCUS ON THE FEW TO IMPACT THE MANY

We are to take the good news of Jesus to the highways, hedges, and to the ends of the Earth. There are many examples in Scripture and throughout history of how little changes can have a big impact. Most major movements and spiritual awakenings have started with one person or a small group. It has been a joy to introduce people to Jesus, then discover later their impact on others. The reproducing life of the Lord Jesus in and through our humanity produces lasting fruit. As followers of Jesus, we can trust that the Holy Spirit will connect us with those who have prepared hearts.

It is valuable to know what it means to be salt and light—realize that we can be part of reproducing and multiplying spiritual movements anywhere, anytime. Every member of the Body of Christ has the capacity and opportunity to participate in Church multiplication, just like the early disciples. It's nothing new.

In orality training with Living Water International, they have observed that God often uses the most unlikely people to spread the good news of Jesus. Sometimes all it takes is a spark that ignites a movement of reproducing communities of Jesus' followers. My longtime friend, Dick Eastman, recently shared with a group at the Jericho Center in Colorado Springs on spiritual awakenings that every major movement of God throughout history started with a few praying people. He noted from research by scholar and historian J. Edwin Orr that on average, these awakenings started with *eleven* people throughout Church history.

Walter was on the wait staff at a hotel conference center where I was scheduled to speak at a men's breakfast. As is my custom, I usually show up early at these kinds of meetings. Before the men began to arrive, I spoke with Walter and shared the Gospel with him. We had prayer together, and he received Christ.

As the guest speaker at the breakfast meeting, I was asked to speak on personal evangelism. As I spoke to the group, I used my encounter with Walter as an example of sharing Christ in those situations. As I mentioned his name, he entered the room with a tray of food. He thought I was introducing him, so he spontaneously began sharing his testimony. It was an amazing reinforcement of my message.

In subsequent years, I have heard from friends who attend the weekly men's breakfast at that hotel. I was told that Walter had been promoted to catering manager, has an outstanding reputation, and is an effective witness to their staff and customers. It is always encouraging to get reports of how God continues to work in the hearts and lives of those we witness to. It's a confirmation of the words of the Apostle Paul from Philippians 1:6, "Being confident of this, that He who began a good work in you will carry it to completion until the day of Christ Jesus."

While it was not an organized team effort, Walter's conversion and spiritual growth was influenced by several people. The men that met at that hotel conference facility for prayer and Bible study had regular contact and an opportunity for nurturing and encouraging Walter in his walk with the Lord.

CONCLUSION

Teamwork is a major part of success in any group, or organization. Jesus' prayer, recorded in John 17, that we, as His body, might become one and come to complete unity is something we can count on. Jesus's prayers get answered! That should inspire us to press on, believing He will make that a reality. Another aspect of teamwork in the Kingdom of God is to consider how some sow, others water, and yet still others reap the harvest. However, it is God who gives the increase.

Chapter 5

How To Be Prepared for the Unexpected

OUR UNCONSCIOUS WITNESS

Alertness and observation are qualities that will help us recognize needs in other people's lives. As we have an attitude of expecting God to work in various circumstances will also help prepare us for the unexpected.

While visiting with a friend at his car dealership, I shared the gospel and led a young man to Christ over a phone conversation. Immediately afterward, I noticed a lady sitting in the dealership's reception area, and I asked her if she had come to a relationship with the Lord. She said yes, so I asked her when. She said it was when she overheard my conversation with the man on the phone a few minutes earlier that she prayed to receive Christ as I was praying with him. Many times we may not be aware of how God uses what say to impact people's lives.

While waiting to catch a plane at a major airport, I engaged a fellow traveler in conversation about spiritual matters. Simply asking a few general non-threatening questions opened the door to ask about the man's spiritual interests. Of course, that led to more personal and penetrating questions and sharing the Gospel. Later, while on the plane, another passenger who overheard our conversation about the Lord said, "I know I should be sharing my faith as you were earlier." This is another example of how God often uses what we say and do to inspire others without our awareness of it.

GOD USES ORDINARY PEOPLE

It is liberating and encouraging to realize that God can use each of us to impact those around us. We don't need to have any special knowledge, a certain position, or special skills. God has put it within each of us, as His followers, to be salt, light, and instruments of change. Jesus once asked a blind beggar, "What do you want me to do for you?" This encounter, recorded in Mark 10, is one of the stories we use in our orality training workshops. After learning, retelling, and discussing the story, a lady in a recent workshop considered the question, how would I respond if Jesus asked me, "What do you want me to do for you?" Almost every true believer would probably respond by saying, "I want to be used by God, to make a difference in the world, and be part of advancing the Kingdom of God."

God puts it in the hearts of His children to want to honor Him, please Him, and walk in His ways. It's part of being a new creation in Christ. We have a new Spirit and new motivation. When we delight ourselves in the Lord, He will give us the desires of our hearts. Of course, God works in us to will and do for His good pleasure. I heard a quote from a Bible teacher years ago: "If it pleases you to do only and always those things that please God, you can do as you please." Another mentor of mine used to say, "Love God and do as we like." It can be liberating to live out this truth.

During difficult times, we must also think about how our lifestyles and behavior can influence those around us. Even if we are not aware of it, we are demonstrating our faith or sometimes failing to do so. The Psalmist tells us to make known the righteous acts of God, to declare His wondrous deeds. The Lord Jesus desires that we show and share His love and truth at every opportunity. This is another way to think about integral mission.

NEW PERSPECTIVES AND INSIGHTS

Over my years of walking with the Lord, I've discovered that engaging in small groups, and discussing important issues, can give a new perspective and insight. In orality training, people gain a new passion and excitement for sharing Christ and advancing the Kingdom of God. Sharing our stories and experiences in small groups can inspire us to do likewise. Years ago, I had the experience of being part of what we called a "blind spot fellowship." We all have blind spots, and sometimes others can see them more clearly than we see ourselves. That approach can be instrumental in discipling and encouraging one another. It helps when we have trusting relationships so that there can be transparency and openness.

The Lord often uses our difficult experiences to improve relationships and build community. We should always be learning how to better respond to people and circumstances. Scripture teaches us to be kind and loving to people and rejoice in all circumstances with thanksgiving. God's design allows His people to live and share in the community. That, of course, can take on many forms of expression. It could be hanging out at a coffee shop, a home, a restaurant, a corporate boardroom, or even getting together under trees in West Africa.

Asking good questions can have a powerful impact in gaining insight. For example, in relation to the work of the Church and missions, many people have different understandings based on culture, traditions, and other factors. The experience of the orality movement is that deep and profound insights can come from learning Bible stories, asking questions, and engaging in group discussions. The following are a few questions that can produce important insights:

1. What is a Church?
2. Why do Churches exist?
3. What is a disciple? How does one become a disciple?
4. What is the Great Commission, and whose responsibility is it?
5. How did Jesus make disciples? Can we make disciples the way He did?
6. What should be our highest priority as followers of Jesus?
7. How can we experience a fruitful and victorious life?
8. What is the role of the Holy Spirit in the believer's life today?

These are all important questions that can bring significant change when we seriously consider them, not based on contemporary religious traditions, but based on what we can or should learn from Jesus, Scripture and the Early Church. Why has the work of God become so complicated and complex when Jesus made it clear, simple, and understandable? We in the modern western world should be rethinking, and sometimes unlearning and relearning, certain things we have often taken for granted. This is an effective exercise to prepare us to witness and minister cross-culturally.

In a recent conversation with a Bible scholar, we discussed some of these questions. His response was, "I haven't thought about that. No one has ever asked me those questions." Sometimes we need to think outside of our cultural and traditional models and think more in terms of a biblical framework. We gain new perspectives when we focus on what we learn from Scripture and the teachings and examples of Jesus. This process helps us get our message and methods into a form that can benefit the least and last unreached people of the world. Essentialism is a term we are hearing more these days, and I believe it is an important conversation to have relating to disciple making.

PRAYER AND THE WORK OF THE SPIRIT

The experience gleaned in the orality movement is that these methods and principles of telling stories by word of mouth are effective anywhere and with all people. Prayer and the work of the Holy Spirit, of course, are foundational to all witness and ministry efforts. He is creative and unlimited in the ways He can draw people to Himself and thrust them into the harvest. A prominent pastor and leader of a network of Churches who participated in an orality training for trainers wrote, "Thank you for this training; it has been a real eye-opener and given us fresh vision for how the Gospel can spread throughout our nation."

My longtime friend Dick Eastman has said, "When God's work becomes too complicated and expensive, we may need to reevaluate whether the Lord is in it or not." A former pastor of mine used to say that our main focus should be loving people and telling them the truth. There seems to be a lost art of simplicity in our modern world and a need to regain an understanding of the power of simplicity and the power of the Gospel.

As I have traveled and ministered in many parts of the world, there is a greater awareness of the need to simplify, streamline and focus our time and resources on the highest-impact activities. Of course, that means different things to different people, depending on context, culture, and worldview. However, with the Word of God and the direction of the Holy Spirit, we can have confidence that we can know and pursue His will. As we act on the Word of God, the Holy Spirit will make course corrections, but we must move first; we must act in faith in His revealed Word.

The Lord delights in answering our questions and answering our prayers. One of the reasons that King David was known as a man after God's own heart is because he was constantly inquiring of the Lord. It would be valuable for each of us to follow his lead. In fact, The Lord tells us to come to His throne of grace and find help in times of need. It's great to keep in mind also that the bigger the need, the bigger the opportunity for God to intervene.

THE POWER OF LISTENING

When we reach out to share the Gospel with someone, it is important to discover a little of the background of the person first. Learning a little about their religious orientation and spiritual belief system is very helpful. Finding out what they already know is better than assuming we know what they need to know. While everyone needs to know and understand the essentials about the person and work of Jesus, it can be communicated in various ways. For example, I have witnessed too many people over the years who have been in Church all their lives. Yet they have never trusted Jesus personally. That is a very different conversation than engaging someone who has never heard the name of Jesus or would not know what a Bible is.

Asking the right questions and listening can save time and enable you to get to the heart of the matter. Sometimes it's simply discovering what people already know about the Lord and filling in the gaps. When a person has little or no knowledge of the Christian faith, it is important to give some background and context before asking them to respond to the message of salvation. Many encounters will be an opportunity to sow the seed of the Word of God into a person's life.

Other times we can water the seed that someone else has already sown. Then some have heard the Gospel and know many truths from the Scriptures but have never personally confessed, believed, and called on the Lord. In all cases, we must seek direction and discernment from the Lord.

Of all the people I have shared the Gospel and prayed with over the years, I would expect that some of those probably did not actually experience the new birth. That is an area out of our control and not really our responsibility. When we communicate the good news of Jesus and trust the Holy Spirit for the results, we can have confidence that He will bear witness to His word. The Holy Spirit's role is to convict and convert lost souls. It is our responsibility to bear witness, share, and show Jesus' love and message. When we do so, we can expect the Holy Spirit will bear witness to His word.

CONCLUSION

When we walk by faith, not sight, and trust God, we can certainly expect the unexpected. That's part of the joy and adventure of being in union with Christ and being on mission with God. In fact, the Lord desires to show Himself strong on our behalf when our hearts are totally yielded to Him. The greater awareness we have of the character and attributes of God, the greater will be our expectance for Him to work in unexpected ways in the hearts and lives of those we engage and in the lives of those we love and pray for, as well as in our own lives.

Chapter 6

What are Divine Appointments and How to Recognize Them

A HOT DOG, AN APPLE, AND A PRAYER

My friend and co-worker Lewis and I had a break between meetings in Washington, D.C. So, we decided to linger in Lafayette Park near the White House for a while. We observed a man going through garbage cans in the park, looking for food. We approached him and introduced ourselves. His name was Columbus, and he shared a bit of his story and how he came to D.C. He came to the city four years earlier, hoping to find a job but ended up homeless and living on the streets.

Lewis and I bought Columbus a hot dog and an apple from a street vendor. We sat with him on a park bench while he ate and he shared more of his story of what his life had been like over the past few years. We were also able to share the Gospel with him and had prayer with him. The Lord had obviously prepared his heart as he joyfully embraced the Gospel and called on the Lord to come into his life and make him a new person.

We needed contact information to follow up with him. So, we came up with an alternative plan. I gave Columbus the contact information for a friend, Major James Hipps with the Salvation Army. About a year later, I reconnected with Major Hipps at a convention in the city. I told him about our encounter with Columbus the year before and asked if he ever showed up at his place. He said he did show up. In fact, he was now overseeing one of the Salvation Army's mission centers in the city. His life was radically transformed as a result of our encounter with him in the park and receiving Christ into his life. This was obviously a divine appointment.

AMBASSADORS FOR CHRIST

Divine appointments can come in many different forms. The main thing is to pay attention to the people and circumstances around us. Praying and trusting God to prepare people's hearts, give us sensitivity, and cause us to be open to the Holy Spirit's leading are all important. A few other simple things can increase the possibility of recognizing those opportunities. Making eye contact, smiling, being friendly, and greeting people will enhance our efforts. Being aware that we are ambassadors for Christ, ministers of reconciliation, and agents of change are vital to the process.

As we pray and ask the Lord to direct our paths and connect us to those who need Him, we can fully expect He will answer those prayers. It's also important to pray and trust God to give us a discerning heart and sensitivity to the people and circumstances we encounter. The Lord Jesus came into the world to seek and save the lost. He now lives in us to carry out that purpose, to be visible expressions of His life and character.

Over the years, as I have spoken about sharing the Gospel and making disciples, sometimes people have expressed an interest in observing firsthand how it works. I have often made offers to go to places where we can interact with people. It could be a shopping mall, a medical center, an airport, a restaurant, or any number of other public locations. On one of those occasions, a young man went with me for such an outing to watch for witness and ministry opportunities. We had lunch at a restaurant in a hotel convention center and engaged a few people in conversations. When departing the restaurant, a lady who was part of the maintenance crew, down on her knees scraping gum off the sidewalk. Prompted by the Holy Spirit, I believe, I approached her, gently put my hand on her shoulder, and said, "You know, while you are down on your knees, this would be an excellent time for you to repent of your sins and receive the Lord Jesus into your life."

There was a pause, then I said, "You know that's what you need, don't you?"

She responded, "Yes, I know I need the Lord."

I said, "Are you aware of the fact that the Lord Jesus came into the world, lived a perfect and sinless life, and died on the cross to pay for your sins?"

Further discussion revealed that the lady had heard and knew about the Gospel but had never responded personally. So, we encouraged her to pray with us and confess her faith in Christ, which she did.

As we were on our way, the man with me said, "Wow, I've never seen that approach before." I had to admit I had never done that before myself. It was an example of how the Holy Spirit might lead us to do something out of the ordinary. The more we respond to the Holy Spirit's prompting, the greater our confidence will be in His willingness to lead and direct our steps and actions.

Being alert and intentional are key factors in recognizing those divine appointments. I practice and encourage others to think ahead of time and pray for divine guidance. When we know we will be connecting and interacting with others, it is important to determine ahead of time that we will take advantage of opportunities to reach out, initiate conversations and trust God to intervene in those situations. He is more than able and ready to use us when we are available to Him.

A DEFINING MOMENT

So often over the years I have experienced how some seemingly random encounter can turn out to be a significant witness opportunity. While on a road trip a few years ago, I came upon a road construction site. A road worker approached my car and explained that there would be about a five-to-ten-minute delay. The Holy Spirit seemed to prompt me to share the Gospel with the worker. My first thought was, 'I don't have time.' Then my next thought, which I believe came from the Lord, was, 'How much time does it take?' I got the message, so I asked the road workers the following question, "Have you noticed any signs of spiritual awakening in this part of the country?"

He responded by saying, "What do you mean?"

I replied, "Have you noticed how many people these days are coming to an awareness of their need for the Lord?"

The road worker said, "I don't know about anybody else, but I know I need the Lord."

That brief exchange opened an opportunity to share the Gospel with the man and discover his eagerness to hear more about Jesus and what it means to know and follow Him. God had obviously prepared the man's heart. I explained more about what it means to believe, confess, and call on the Lord from Romans 10. I sensed that the Holy Spirit was dealing with his heart, so I suggested that we include the Lord in our conversation and encouraged him to call on the Lord and confess his faith in Him, which he did. When we finished praying, the worker at the other end of the construction site signaled to proceed. So, I gave him a Gospel booklet and was on my way.

Interestingly, as I was driving that day before reaching the construction site, I was meditating on the Scripture where Jesus said, "The words that I speak, are Spirit and Life." The Lord seemed to impress on me that the words that I speak, prompted by the Holy Spirit, can produce life in others. The more conscious we are that our words have the power to change lives, the greater will be our confidence to speak words of life to others. Divine appointments sometimes only need to be recognized as such

CONCLUSION

It is safe to assume that every human contact is a potential divine appointment. Suppose we really believe that God is working all things together for our good and His glory and purposes. In that case, divine appointments are a natural part of our everyday interactions with others. The important question is, will we take action, step out in faith and say something to the people the Lord brings across our paths? I am continually amazed at how God often brings me across people who are open and have prepared hearts. We seldom know how the Lord works in someone's life until we engage them in conversation.

Chapter 7

What it Takes to Attain Long-Lasting and Generational Impact

THE POWER OF THE NAME OF JESUS

Nassar was an Iranian service station worker where I regularly stopped to buy gas. After a few casual conversations, I asked Nassar about his interest in spiritual things and if he had a relationship with God. Nassar came from a Muslim family and country but was not practicing. He told me about a businessman who was traveling through the city and gave him a Bible a few years earlier. He had started reading some but said he didn't understand it. Of course, that led to a conversation about the person and work of Jesus. After further discussion and explanation about the plan of God and the Gospel, he was open to responding and receiving Christ into his life. I gave him another book to read and encouraged him to continue reading his Bible. I stayed in touch with him and continued to have follow-up conversations with him from time to time.

In subsequent weeks I invited him to visit the Church where I was a member. It was an eye-opener for Nassar because he had never been inside a Church. He began sharing his testimony and became very bold in his witness to his co-workers and customers at the service station. Late one night, there was an attempt by a man to rob the service station.

Nassar asked the man this question, "Do you know God?"

The man said, "No."

Nassar said, "Sit down and let me tell you about Jesus."

When Nassar told me about that encounter later, Nassar said, "I preached unto him, Jesus." He had been reading the Gospels and the Book of Acts and believed that God could work now as He did then. It was obviously a divine intervention in that the man responded to the message and the name of Jesus, and he did not rob the station. It was a real demonstration of the authority the Lord has given us and the power in the Name of Jesus. From time to time, Nassar would tell me about other witness and ministry opportunities he had. He led the owner of the service station to the Lord. The owner's wife had seen a real change in her husband's life. At a company get-together, she asked Nassar, "Whatever you did to my husband, can you do it to my son as well?"

In the following months after Nassar came to the Lord, he led one of his brothers and a cousin back in Iran to the Lord in a phone conversation. His brother eventually became a pastor. In subsequent years I received reports of how the Lord worked in his family. Several of his family members, relatives, and friends came to faith in Christ through his and his family's witness. His brother, who became a pastor, was later imprisoned for preaching the Gospel. A sister-in-law and a nephew had to flee the country because of their Christian faith and were refugees in Turkey for a period of time. It is amazing and encouraging to see how the Lord uses those who have very limited knowledge of the Bible or theology but have a basic understanding of the person and work of Jesus and boldly share Him with others.

REPRODUCING DISCIPLE-MAKING

Sometimes there is no human explanation for the redemptive work of the Holy Spirit and how he uses every situation and anyone available to Him. It is encouraging to realize that God is always at work everywhere to redeem His creation and that each of us can be a part of what He is doing.

In the Spring of 1969, as a freshman in college, I was introduced to the idea of selling books door-to-door as a summer job. Raymond Francis convinced me that if I studied, worked hard, and followed instructions, I could earn a lot of money. That turned out to be true, and I enjoyed a five-year journey with The Southwestern Company. In addition to putting my wife and myself through college, the experience was more valuable than the money in the long run.

Learning to meet and deal with all kinds of people, managing time and money, and other disciplines have been extremely helpful. Communication, management, and leadership skills have also benefited my academic and business endeavors, and ministry and mission activities. My Southwestern experience introduced me to numerous ideas, resources, mentors, and friends. Many of those I've maintained contact with over the years. One of those is a fellow bookman, Jim Potts, a successful businessman and owner of Lewis and Clark Outfitters based in Northwest Arkansas. Several years ago, Jim shared an idea that stuck in my mind. He said he likes to focus on "introducing people to people and people to opportunities." That may seem like a simple concept, but it has profound implications and applications.

In the early 1990s, I was introduced to a man named Landon Short soon after moving to Houston. He has since gone on to be with the Lord. Landon had the reputation of being a master networker. He was the first to arrive and the last to leave meetings, in which he attended and participated a lot. He would be heard saying, "I want you to meet someone." He was very intentional about introducing people and facilitating relationships. As a result of my relationship with Landon, I got to know many of his friends and associates throughout the Greater Houston area. In today's corporate culture, he would be known as a "super-connector." Super-connectors are recognized as some of the most strategic and valuable people within various businesses, organizations, Churches and ministries.

Several years ago, I heard the late Dr. Ralph Winter, renowned missiologist and founder of the US Center for World Mission (now Frontier Ventures), say that one of the most important and strategic roles in the Church/mission world is the partnership facilitator. Getting people to work together is not easy but is a very worthwhile endeavor. Networking, collaboration, and partnerships are big business, education, and the Church topics. In fact, the decade of the 2020s has been designated as the Decade of Collaboration by the leadership of Mission Nexus, which is made up of several hundred organizations.

So many simple activities anyone can engage in have a major impact. Making introductions, cultivating relationships, and maintaining friendships are incredibly important to maximize our witness and ministry efforts. A few years ago, a long-time friend and colleague in the ministry told me about a meeting with one of Southeast Asia's most successful Church/mission leaders and prayer mobilizers. When asked about the key to his success, this man said, "I make friends." Making and keeping friends is sometimes a challenge but is a worthwhile endeavor. It's one of the most important aspects of effective leadership. While knowledge and skill are important, it's the character that sustains friendships and relationships and produces fruitfulness in the long run.

JESUS, THE MODEL DISCIPLE MAKER

The most important introduction we can make is introducing people to Jesus. Over the years, people have told me they don't have the gift of evangelism. However, it's not a gift, but the Gospel is the power of God unto salvation. These days we have many resources and tools to aid us in communicating the Gospel, introducing others to Jesus, and making disciples. In addition to personal conversations and engagement with people, we can give them a Bible or Gospel literature or refer them to a digital resource. Years ago, I came across a quote, "God uses tracts, do you?" Of course, we know He uses all forms of communication. The simplest, most economical, and very likely the most effective way of introducing others to Jesus is personally telling our story and God's story.

One of the features that makes Bible storying, orality training, and oral art forms so powerful is its simplicity and reproducibility. The most basic thing that works everywhere is asking questions and telling stories. When we ask good questions and listen to other people's stories, they will often ask to hear our story, which can lead to sharing God's story. When followers of Jesus are properly trained in the concepts and principles of orality, they can take the Gospel to any place and people group on the planet. Over the years, with Living Water International's orality training programs, we have focused on equipping people with just what is in their heads and hearts that can be reproduced in the heads and hearts of others, requiring no written material or technology. Of course, when available and culturally appropriate, we want to use all means available, including print-based and various electronic and digital media resources.

Our orality training emphasizes the value of learning a little, practicing a lot, implementing immediately, and telling stories often. It is better to know a little that we share a lot and with many than to know a lot that we keep to ourselves. We like to say, "Keep the Faith; just don't keep it to yourself." Biblical storytelling and oral methods enable us to do so with great impact. These methods and strategies are not new. In fact, orality-based methods and strategies are the most effective ways people have learned and communicated from the beginning. It is the way Jesus communicated, instructed, and equipped His followers. He often used parables and stories, asked questions, and created community and relationships.

Years ago, it was a revolutionary discovery to realize that the same God who lived in Jesus Christ more than 2,000 years ago now lives in me. He lives in every believer who has been born of the Spirit. Christ in us is the hope of glory, we are told in Colossians 1:27. This truth should be a transformational experience for every follower of Jesus. It's not the super deluxe version of the Christian life, but the truth about each of us who belong to Him. Galatians 2:20 tells us it is no longer us living, but Christ living in us. Awareness of these realities should motivate us to share His life with all we can.

These truths are not referring to heaven someday but a present reality of Christ now living in us. Heaven will be glorious, but the hope of glory is about the glory of God is real and seen in our lives now. One of my mentors used to say, "When the glory of God is in your life, you'll have to backslide to keep from winning others to Christ." God wants His glory and righteousness to be visible and demonstrated in all of His children. When that is a reality in our lives, our words and testimonies will have a greater impact.

CONDITIONS FOR REVIVAL

Many parallels can be found when we study the major revivals and spiritual awakenings recorded throughout the Bible, as well as in Church history. They normally happen during crises, hardships, and difficult times. Significant movements of God resulted in activating the Body of Christ as multitudes turned to the Lord. There are many lessons and principles that should encourage each of us as followers of Jesus. I was recently in conversation with a friend who is a Bible scholar and historian. He was sharing some of the conditions that existed just before the First and Second Great Awakenings in the United States. Things were very bad. There was a lot of turbulence, spiritual darkness, corruption, and moral decay. There are many parallels between cultural issues and societal conditions between then and now. The moral and spiritual decline sets the stage for renewal, revival, and spiritual awakening, and increasing numbers of people come to an awareness of their need for the Lord.

In the decade of the 1980s, there were several pockets of awakenings and significant movements. A major prayer gathering of more than a million people took place in South Korea during the summer of 1984. It was just prior to the Summer Olympic Games in southern California. A lot of prayer and preparation went into the Olympic Outreach Coalition. More than seventy mission groups and denominations and 1,800 Churches in the region participated in that outreach effort. We heard reports the crime rate in Los Angles was the lowest during that two-week period than it had been in modern history. It was estimated that more than 1,000 people responded to the Gospel every day during the Games. Dr. Ralph Winter, the founder of Frontier Ventures (then known as the US Center for World Mission), said, "It was the most lavish outpouring of effective, well-organized, evangelical attention to any event in history."

The 1984 Olympic Outreach was a catalyst and set in motion several other worldwide movements over the next several years. With more than 200 organizations, the Winning Way Coalition was birthed in the Fall of that year. Then following on the heels of those efforts, the International Bible Reading Association was formed in 1988, resulting in 1990 being declared the **International Year of Bible Reading** by a congressional resolution, followed by a presidential proclamation by President George H.W. Bush. A few other presidents and heads of state around the world also issued similar proclamations. Bible reading marathons and prayer vigils were conducted in various places around the world. A Bible Reading Marathon was conducted on the Mount of Olives in Jerusalem, then to Berlin, Washington DC, and many other cities. College and university campuses also hosted Bible reading marathons and prayer vigils.

In 1995, Seoul, South Korea, was the host city for the Global Consultation for World Evangelization (GCOWE '95). It was one of several gatherings connected with the AD 2000 and Beyond Movement. During those meetings, I had the opportunity of spending some time with Dr. Robert Coleman. Of the many books he has authored, he had just finished his latest at that time, titled *The Coming World Revival*. Dr. Coleman has written extensively over the years about revivals and spiritual awakenings. He has said, "Scripture seems to allude to a world revival, though this interpretation is by no means unanimous."

It was also in 1995 that God sparked revival and awakening on the campuses of several colleges, universities, and a few seminaries around the country. Beginning at Howard Payne University, as well as Houston Baptist University, the move of the Spirit eventually spread to more than fifty campuses around the country. Several articles and books were written during that season, giving accounts of how the Lord was at work. There was much brokenness, repentance, and open confession that seemed to be contagious. All those movements accelerated the spreading of the Gospel.

Increasing numbers of Church and mission leaders are sensing that we could be on the verge of the next Great Awakening, and many are praying and believing in it. Renewals, revivals, and awakenings can take on many different forms of expression, and they may not look like past movements. They can be personal or corporate. It is wonderful to be part of a corporate move of God. However, we don't have to wait for some sweeping move of God. We can enter into His redemptive activities at any time. He is ready when we are and is prepared to renew us, fill us, and use us when we seek Him with our whole hearts.

CONCLUSION

A concept that has been helpful to me over the years is to think of relational network clusters. We may not be connected to a vast number of close relationships. However, consider those we are in a relationship with and the number of connections those people are related to or connected with. When we have a spiritual influence on one person, it can have a ripple effect and a multiplying impact on many others. Think of generational impact as sowing seed. An illustration we often talk about is the fact that you can count the seeds in an apple, but you can't count the apples in a seed.

Chapter 8

How to Become a Movement Mobilizer

QUESTIONS TO PONDER

Consider what it takes to ignite a movement, build a business, or grow a Church or an organization. What are the principles, methods, or strategies that enable each of us, as followers of Jesus, to make an impact on the Kingdom of God? There are some very simple and understandable answers. We also have many examples throughout the Bible and throughout history that should encourage us that God can use us in these ways today. The more we are aware of how the Lord has worked throughout history, the greater should be our confidence that He can do the same works through us today. Jesus is the same yesterday, today, and forever.

An example in Church history is Daniel Nash (1775-1831), who served as his personnel intercessor with the renowned evangelist Charles Finney. He was key to the revival that followed Finney's ministry. We can all look at the life of Daniel Nash and see an example of how important prayer is in advancing the Kingdom of God. When God would direct where a meeting was to be held, Nash would quietly go into the town and seek to get two or three people to join in a covenant of prayer with him.

The lives and influence of those like Nash should inspire each of us, that each of us can become movement mobilizers. Scripture affirmed that we have access to the throne of grace and are invited to come to Him in times of need. From God's perspective, the greater the need, the greater the opportunity. Where sin abounds, grace much more abounds. It should give us hope to know that God often does some of His greatest work in the darkest places and in the most difficult times.

It should encourage us to realize that God can use each of us to be movement mobilizers. It could start with a conversation, a prayer for some chance encounter.

A DEFINING MOMENT

A few years ago, I reconnected with my friend Brian who I had some ministry with more than thirty years ago. We were together in Washington, D.C., after attending a White House briefing waiting for a taxi on a nearby sidewalk. It was raining, and a kind lady standing nearby offered to share her umbrella with us. While we waited for the taxi, I engaged her in conversation, asked a few questions, and shared the Gospel with her. She was interested and open, and we had prayer together, and she confessed her faith in Jesus. The whole encounter took less than ten minutes.

I did not realize it at the time, but that experience had a profound impact on Brian. It inspired him to become more intentional and proactive about sharing the Gospel. A few years ago, Brian and I reconnected at a convention, and he told me that he has continued to share his faith regularly. He said that, on average, he had seen two or three people a week respond to the Lord and confess their faith in Christ since that encounter on the sidewalk more than thirty years earlier. Brian is a great example of how the Lord honors His Word as we sow it into the lives of others.

Brian told me later that a couple of questions I asked the lady that day captured his attention, and he was inspired to use them many times. Those questions concerned how I opened the conversation and how I drew the net or closed the conversation. Those questions were the following:

"I bet you've been thinking more about the Lord lately, haven't you?"

Then after briefly sharing the Gospel, ask this closing question:

"Can you think of any reason why you wouldn't want to receive Christ into your life right now?"

There are so many other simple questions we can ask to open potential life-changing conversations. There are also numerous ways of inviting people to respond after we have shared the Gospel. Simply saying something like, "We can include the Lord in our conversation, and you can call upon Him right now." It's usually helpful to explain believing, confessing, and calling on the Lord as described in Romans 10. Being flexible and trusting the Holy Spirit to give us His tailor-made approach and close is vital. He may lead us to do or say things that are new and different, things we have not been trained to say or do but are still in line with Scripture. Notice how Jesus often said or did things out of the ordinary.

During the Jesus Movement of the early 1970s, a lyric from Kurt Kaiser's song "Pass It On" became very popular. The lyric went: "**It only**

takes a spark to get a fire going."[2] Many students were ignited with great passion during those days for sharing the Gospel on college and university campuses around the country. In fact, that song has had an impact around the world. In 2015, while conducting an orality training for pastors in Zimbabwe, I happened to mention that song. One of the pastors in the training spontaneously began singing the first verse of the song, and others knew the words and joined in.

It is remarkable and worth reminding ourselves of how one person, moved by the Holy Spirit, can gain a passion and become active in sharing Christ. Only the Lord knows the multiplying impact one transformed life can have on many others over time.

PRINCIPLES OF THE KINGDOM

Think about the principles that enable each of us, as followers of Jesus, to make the greatest possible contribution to advancing the Kingdom of God. These are important questions to ponder, and I suggest there are some simple and understandable answers. The parables of mustard seed and yeast that Jesus talked about are examples of these Kingdom principles that can become catalysts to start movements that can change the world. These parables show us that little things can have a major impact. The new Testament examples include the Samaritan Woman at the Well, the demon-possessed Gerasene, and Phillip's encounter with the Ethiopian eunuch. These show how God can use one person to impact a community, a region, or even an entire nation.

In the natural realm, consider that every major river starts with a small stream. A small snowball can cause an avalanche. A seed is the begin-

---

2 Kurt Kaiser, "Pass it On," 1969, *The United Methodist Hymnal*, No. 572, Communiqué Music.

ning of a tree that produces much fruit. The late Dr. Avery Willis, renowned missiologist and founder of the International Orality Network, had a favorite saying, "You can count the seeds in an apple, but you can't count the apples in a seed." Consider how many major corporations started out in someone's kitchen or garage. Megachurches and major Church planting/disciple-making movements have started in living rooms, storefronts, and under trees.

In the 1970s and '80s, a few missionaries and Church leaders became interested and began discussing orality. Those discussions were about how to reach the Bible-less people groups, oral cultures, and oral preference learners. Recent research shows that more than 70 percent of the world's population are oral learners by necessity or preference. It was from those seemingly insignificant and obscure conversations that several things were put in motion. It was during a Lausanne Movement gathering called Amsterdam 2,000 that resulted in the formation of the Oral Bible Task Force, and a few years later became the International Orality Network.

Increasing numbers of mission and ministry leaders, pastors and Church leaders, business professionals, and ordinary followers of Jesus are now paying attention to the orality movement. Some are saying that orality's concepts, principles, and practices could revolutionize how the Church/Mission World communicates the Gospel and makes disciples. Understanding small, simple, and reproducible principles are key factors that can enhance our potential to witness and impact advancement in the Kingdom of God. It's important to think of having a multiplying effect.

POWER OF WATER AND THE WORD

Living Water International is another example of how small beginnings can grow into something big. Beginning with a short-term mission trip from Houston to East Africa in 1990, Living Water International is now considered by many to be the world's leading Great Commission Water Solutions organization. To date, more than 24,000 water projects have been completed, and millions of lives have been saved and transformed since its founding. Clean water saves lives physically, but it's the Living Water that Jesus talked about in John 7 that changes and saves lives for eternity.

Consider from seed to fruit, stream to river, snowball to avalanche. The orality movement is an example of those Kingdom principles being worked out in our time. Based on all the Lord has done over the past forty years, it's exciting to consider all He has in mind for the next forty years. We can all be a part of this historic movement of God in advancing His Kingdom, and the realization of the prophecy of Habakkuk 2:14, "For the Earth will be filled with the knowledge of the glory of the Lord, as the waters cover the sea."

We seldom know how God may work in the lives of those we share with and introduce to the Lord. One transformed life can be a catalyst for a spiritual movement that could impact thousands. It has happened many times throughout history and can happen now. The Lord Jesus is the same yesterday, today, and forever. When we are in the stream of God's redemptive activities, we can expect great things from the Lord.

Scripture tells us we have not because we ask not. The more we ask God for the things He has promised in His Word, the more we can expect to receive. There are so many aspects of prayer that can enhance our efforts and win others to Christ and discipling them on their journey with the Lord.

I have often asked people questions like:

- Do you have a praying grandmother?
- Has anyone been praying for you?
- How can I pray for you?
- Is there anything going on in your life I can pray with you about?

When asking these questions, most people will have something they are willing to share. Then there are many opportunities to follow up and see how the Lord answers prayers. God is especially interested in answering prayers for the felt needs of lost people, so we know He is real and cares. Many become open to the Gospel as a result.

A friend often asks, "What is one thing I can pray with you about right now?" He then prays for them on the spot. Many have come to the Lord with these approaches.

PRAYER OPENS DOORS

When I initiated conversations about prayer, I discovered that people have been prayed for. It is great to know that we can be the answer to someone else's prayers. Most people are not opposed to being prayed for.

God is not willing that any should perish but that all would come to repentance. Jesus came to seek and save the lost, and He now lives in us to carry out that purpose. Our awareness of these truths and our praying according to the will of God can give us great confidence in introducing others to the Lord and nurturing them in their spiritual growth and journey.

One night my friend Charles said over dinner, "I'm tired of plain vanilla Christianity." We were both in Washington, D.C., on business and had a good dinner, sharing about our jobs, ministries, and walks with the Lord. I prayed with Charles about his desire to see the power of God at work in new ways and assured him that the Lord would answer the desire of his heart.

We left the restaurant and decided to walk a few blocks back toward our hotel. As we waited to cross an intersection, Charles struck up a conversation with a man trying to restart his truck. It had broken down as he made a turn and blocked part of our crosswalk. He had diagnosed the problem and called his wife, who was on her way with a part he needed. We waited with him and began to share with him about the Lord Jesus.

"The Lord must have put you in our path tonight so we could tell you about Him," we said. "Both of us have received Jesus Christ into our lives, and it's the most encouraging thing that's ever happened to us. We no longer struggle with guilt over what we know we have done wrong. We have a genuine peace and joy in our lives." After sharing further about the death, burial, and resurrection of the Lord Jesus and God's desire to make him a new person, we asked the man if he would be willing to call on the Lord and receive Christ into his life. The man said yes, and we were praying with him as his wife drove up with the needed part. Their teenage daughter was in the car with her.

While the man began to repair his truck, we shared with his wife, "We've got great news for you! Your husband just received the Lord Jesus into his life. You need to do that, too, don't you?" She said yes, as did the teenage daughter. Within ten or fifteen minutes from the time we came to that intersection, we were standing under the streetlight, our hands joined with those of this family in a circle of prayer. We prayed that their entire family would come to be united in Christ!

We continued toward our hotel and encountered a barefoot man reeling under the influence of liquor and drugs. His jaw had been broken, and his teeth were wired together. He was muttering unintelligible syllables. We finally made out his demand for a cigarette. I thought of what Peter said to the blind man at the Beautiful Gate: *"Silver and gold I do not have, but what I do have I give you"* (Acts 3:6). Neither Charles nor I had a cigarette to give, and the third time the man asked, I looked him straight in the eye and declared with as much authority as I could muster, "I don't have any cigarettes, but I do have something you need. In the name of Jesus Christ—"

Before I could finish the sentence, the man began to cry out, "Oh, no!" He jerked into stunned silence as though something had hit him. I had no doubt it was the power of God. He put out his hands to brace himself against a wall behind him, and a softness began to come over his countenance. I continued to affirm the promises of God over him:

- The Lord Jesus Christ is the King of Kings and the Lord of Lords.
- The Lord Jesus Christ is taking power and authority over the power of the enemy that has been working within you.
- The Lord Jesus Christ has freed you from the torment that has plagued your life.
- The Lord Jesus Christ is available to you right now, and you can call upon His name.

As I spoke, he stood up, and his words became clear. He put on the shoes he had been carrying in his arms and tied the laces; then, we began to walk together.

By now, I had begun reciting the Twenty-third Psalm: *"The Lord is my shepherd; I shall not want ..."* When I got to the line, *"I will fear no evil,"* he joined in, *"'I will fear no evil,"* and repeated that line repeatedly.

"The Lord has released you," I assured him, "from the satanic stronghold that was keeping you in bondage. You can call upon His name now." The man repeated the name *Jesus* softly.

I could tell he needed rest. We hailed a cab and took him to a nearby shelter for a night's lodging. I went into the shelter with him, and Charles stayed in the cab, explaining to the driver—a Muslim from Iran—what had just happened to this man. Charles's face was radiant with joy when I returned. He had led this cab driver to the Lord. The driver said he had never seen such compassion and knew that the power of God in our lives was genuine.

"Plain vanilla?" I asked Charles.

"No way!" Not for Charles. And certainly not for the truck driver and his family, the barefoot homeless man, or the Iranian cab driver. Need a lift in your spiritual life? Share your faith with someone. Introduce others to the living Christ.

When we step out in faith, act on the Word of God, and trust Him, we can expect God to work. It may not be spectacular or sensational, but it will have eternal implications. There is great power in speaking and acting in the name of the Lord Jesus.

CONCLUSION

One of my mentors years ago said, "When God initiates something, He maintains it. When we start something, you must maintain it." That thought has come to my mind many times over the years. It's a good reminder to stay in a spirit of prayer and maintain an attitude of dependence on God, the Holy Spirit. It is important to maintain communion with God in such a way that I can trust that He is initiating and guiding my thoughts and actions. That gives me confidence that God can work through my words and actions to mobilize movements for His Kingdom's impact. Movements of any kind usually begin with one person, then sharing a few, which can grow in numbers over time.

Chapter 9

How Little Things Can Produce a Major Impact and Influence

SURPRISED BY THE WORK OF GOD

In 1967 in Kabul, Afghanistan, I was introduced to some new and different customs and cultural dynamics. Being stationed at an Air Force base in a neighboring country, traveled to several surrounding countries in that part of the world. During those years, I became aware of the geopolitical issues in the region. In subsequent years, I connected with people doing business and mission work in the region. The Lord was using those experiences and relationships to prepare me for something I could not have foreseen at the time.

For most of the 1980s, I worked with an international publishing and broadcasting ministry. During the Soviet Union's invasion of Afghanistan, we were involved in some mission work in the same region. In partnership and collaboration with medical and relief organizations, distributed Bibles, and Gospel literature among the Mujahideen freedom fighters and in the refugee camps of Northwest Pakistan. Over the course of those efforts, we made some encouraging and amazing discoveries. The USSR was assigning known Christian troops to duty in Afghanistan, the most undesirable place of service in their military complex.

It was a pleasant surprise to be told that twenty-two Bible studies had been identified as taking place among the Afghan people in Muslim villages. They were being led by Soviet troops. This was obviously a very turbulent time for the people in that region. When you think of a mission strategy being carried out in a Muslim country during a Marxist revolution, funded by an atheist communist government, it is quite remarkable. Only God could have arranged such an amazing Kingdom expansion effort.

Throughout history, there have been many developments that can only be attributed to the sovereign hand of God. One of my mentors years ago was the missionary statesman and author Norman Grubb. He wrote many books and articles; one of my favorites was titled "*That Clever God.*" Norman was instrumental in starting the first Chapter of Intervarsity Christian Fellowship while a student at Cambridge University. He married the daughter of C. T. Studd and went to the Congo as a missionary in 1919. I often think of his teachings and writings when thinking about reaching people and carrying out God's purposes. He often emphasized the fact that every negative has a positive. Furthermore, the more negative the negative, the more positive the positive. That principle is a good one to keep in mind these days during this global pandemic.

Having vision, strategic plans, goals, and objectives, with metrics and measurements, is necessary and valuable. However, to walk by faith, not by sight, and have flexible plans is also important. In fact, it is good to be prepared for God to intervene, re-direct or change our plans at any time. He often has different, bigger, and better plans than we have. Thankfully, He also has veto power over all our plans and strategies.

NEVER TOO LATE TO SHARE YOUR FAITH

An eighty-four-year-old man attended a Bible storying orality training workshop. He was interested in becoming more effective at sharing his faith. This man had been a believer since his teenage years and a Sunday School teacher for more than sixty years. After the training, he said, "I wish somebody would have taught me this seventy years ago."

One of the stories that participants learn is the story of Nicodemus, from John 3. The eighty-four-year-old man had a doctor's appointment and had determined ahead of time that he would look for an opportunity to tell the story and share his faith. In the doctor's office, there was a woman he could engage in conversation with. He asked the woman if he could tell her a story he had recently learned. She said yes. He introduces the story by telling her it's about being born again. Before he could get into the story, the woman stopped him and said, **"Wait a minute, I need to be born again."** So, the man briefly shared the Gospel and invited her to pray with him. She confessed her faith in Christ and invited Him to come into her life.

Sometimes, God has already prepared their hearts when we step out in faith and engage people in spiritual conversations. As we pray and ask God for those opportunities, we can fully expect He will answer those prayers. I'm often amazed and surprised to see how the Lord orchestrates those connections for His Kingdom's purposes. A key factor is simply asking, believing, stepping out in faith, and acting on what we believe is the Spirit's leading.

The man later said, "I didn't even get to tell the story." Well, that experience illustrates how the Holy Spirit is creative and unlimited in the ways He can use us to have a spiritual impact on others. It's also a good reminder that when we have the desire to be used by God, He will make a way to fulfill that desire. Our ability is not as important as our availability. When we are available to the Lord and trusting Him, He will often work in unexpected ways.

Psalm 92 is a great Chapter that helps us understand that followers of Jesus can still bear fruit in old age. I'm reminded of a very dear friend who passed away a few years ago. During a series of hospital stays, he was able to share the Gospel and pray with a good number of nurses, aides, and others. Several were open to the Lord and confessed Christ as my friend shared with them from his hospital bed. Another friend has a ministry of equipping and encouraging people to '*Finish Well.*' He likes to say we are not done until we're dead, and if we have a pulse, we have a purpose.

ORALITY AND EVERYDAY LIVING

Having been involved in the orality movement over the years, I am increasingly aware of how people learn, communicate, process information, and remember things. In our orality training, we emphasize that when we use orality-based communication methods, we use a different part of our brains than when we read texts. Studies show that storytelling and other oral art forms activate our brains and enhance memory. Of course, everybody can benefit from having a better memory. It's not so much about how much we read or learn, or how many degrees we've earned, but what we remember that changes our lives and makes us more productive in every part of life.

Remember, or some form of that word, is the second most given command throughout all of Scripture. When I make that statement, sometimes people ask, "What is the most given command?" The first most given command is, "Do not be afraid, or fear not." We can only live out what we can remember. So, communicating so people remember is important. If you think about it, the most effective communicators are usually good storytellers.

One of the observations we made several years ago in an orality training in Liberia was how people responded and retained information. In a Bible storying workshop with more than one hundred people, about half of the participants had their Bibles, notepads, and pens, while the other half had none, as they were non-literate or oral learners. At the end of the training day, we observed that the oral learners could learn and retell the stories better than the literate participants. The oral learners were more accustomed to hearing, discussing, and repeating the stories, whereas the literate ones depended more on text-based methods. It is important to note that even among highly educated and literate populations, orality-based methods can enhance the learning experience and the ability to retain information.

THE MOTHER OF ALL LEARNING

It may seem like common knowledge, but it is valuable to practice a well-known concept. That is, "Repetition is the mother of all learning." Our training strategies emphasize the benefits of learning a little, practicing a lot, and telling stories often. It is better to know a little that we share a lot than to know a lot that we keep to ourselves." More repetition, learning in the community, and the use of imagination are great lessons anyone can benefit from. Another advantage of learning in community is we can benefit from the collective memory of the group. It illustrates the importance of living in community and enter-personal relationships.

Some Churches and ministries in North America and the Western World are beginning to discover many lessons we can learn from the more relational, communal, Oral cultures in the Global South. These are also lessons we can learn from the early church as recorded in the book of Acts. In our training efforts, we see barriers come down and trusting relationships built. Some still consider Orality and Storytelling beneficial for non-literate or less educated people. However, the concepts and principles of oral learning are important in areas where individualism and isolationism are prevalent, such as North America.

TRUTH THAT STICKS

When considering communicating the Gospel and Making Disciples, the Arts Community has much to offer. Not only the visual and performing arts for effective communication but also areas such as relational, participatory, and dialogical arts to develop and maintain community. These are valuable skills for everyday life and ministry. Think of the difference between reading a book instead of seeing a movie and discussing it with friends. Consider how the Lord has used the 'Jesus' Film over the years. Then as viewers discuss it in the community, it sticks. The late Dr. Avery Willis, and co-author Mark Snowden do a great job making a case for the power of orality in their book *Truth That Sticks*.

There are many images throughout Scripture that communicate spiritual truths and life principles. The Lord Jesus used many images, like the vine and the branches, the wise man who built his house on a rock, the parable of the Sower, and many others. Jesus is our best model as a communicator, trainer, disciple maker, and leader. Most people in His day were oral Learners, as it is today. Even though more people are literate now, most of the world's population, an estimated eighty percent, would be considered oral learners by necessity or preference. It's not a matter of intelligence or academic training but more about worldview, culture, learning, and communication preferences.

One of the big questions today would be: "How are we going to be able to communicate the Gospel to everyone and make disciples among all people groups?" Another strategic question is, "Can we communicate, train and make disciples the way Jesus did?" The answer to these questions, of course, is "Yes," because the same Holy Spirit is at work in the world today, and each of us, born of the Spirit, has Christ living in us. Consider what it means to be a disciple of Jesus. A disciple is a learner and follower of the Lord Jesus. Once you have introduced someone to Him and they have received His free gift of salvation, you have actually made a disciple.

Being a disciple and becoming a reproducing disciple-maker is a life-long process. When we first become believers and followers of Jesus, we can expect to continue to grow in that relationship and in spiritual maturity. Certainly, we never arrive at perfection but should continue to grow into Christlikeness as long as we are here on earth. We can also be encouraged that the best is yet to be with Christ in our lives.

CONCLUSION

A friend of mine introduced me to a business associate years ago. In the introduction, my friend said, "By the way, Jerry is a believer too." The man I was introduced to said, "Oh great, another fisher of men." In reality, I was not at that time a fisher of men; I was not active in sharing my faith. However, the thought, "Oh great, another fisher of men," stuck in my mind, and the Lord used that statement to motivate me. The Lord often brings to my mind the words of Jesus, "Follow me, and I will make you become fishers of men (people)." So, if we follow Jesus, we can count on the fact that He is making us fishers of people.

Chapter 10

What is The Kingdom of God like

A QUESTION—A TURNING POINT

In Washington, D.C. in 1989, a friend asked me a question, which turned out to be a turning point in my life. She said, "Jerry, have you ever thought about writing a book?" Well, I had, in fact, thought about it, but that was about as far as I had gotten. In retrospect, I believe the Lord had put it in my heart to write a book, but I wasn't sure how to go about it at the time. The lady who asked me that question had heard me speak and had read some articles about my witnessing and ministry journey and thought a book would be beneficial for equipping others. That conversation made my friend connect me with a publisher and an acquisition editor. Then, three years later, my first book, *How to Win Others to Christ,* was released. I can think of several seemingly insignificant events or conversations over the years that have turned out to be important developments.

In 1993, in Houston, Texas, the general manager of a Christian radio network came across my book that had just been released. He reached out to me and requested to do a series of interviews for a broadcast. After recording the interviews, he asked me this question, "Jerry, have you ever thought about producing a radio program?" Again, I had thought about it, but had not acted on that thought. The station manager encouraged me to record a series of audition programs for a short feature radio broadcast. The board of directors for the radio network listened to the audition tapes and agreed to do a ninety-day test of the broadcasts. Well, the ninety-day test resulted in the radio program being on the air three times a day, every weekday, since 1993. The program has also been provided to other media outlets and has been broadcast into 174 countries over the years. These are just a couple of examples of how the principles of the Kingdom of God can work. Little things really can make a big impact.

Jesus said the Kingdom of God is like a mustard seed. It's a very small seed that produces a very large plant. He also said that the Kingdom of God is like yeast. A small amount of yeast can affect a large lump of dough. Jesus spoke to His disciples with many similar parables as much as they could understand. He used many images and pictures to communicate spiritual truth and what the Kingdom of God is like. These parables show us that little things matter and often can have a big impact.

THE TRIMTAB FACTOR

Every aircraft and ocean-going vessel have a rudder. On the tip of the rudder is a smaller rudder known as a trimtab. When the trimtab turns, it turns the rudder, and the rudder turns the plane or ship.

It's a great lesson to know and understand how little things can have a great impact. Knowing how God uses so many ways of advancing His Kingdom and how we can participate in His redemptive activities is also encouraging. There are several other ways of thinking about these Kingdom principles. Strategic resource leveraging and force multipliers are other terms that are often used to describe these concepts.

In the orality movement, we emphasize how God uses all means available for communicating the Gospel, making disciples, and multiplying Church movements. Of all the ways and means He has used and is using; most people have come to the Lord through Orality-based methods. Depending on the culture and context, churches can include cell groups, simple, organic, house Churches, congregations that meet under trees, and many other expressions of the Body of Christ. Sometimes, we may be tempted to think that bigger is always better. However, small, simple, reproducible systems and structures have a greater and longer-lasting impact.

The reproducing life of the Lord Jesus in and through our humanity produces lasting fruit. It could also be the trimtab, strategic resource leveraging, or force multiplying effect. These are all demonstrations of the Kingdom principles of the mustard seed and yeast. As followers of Jesus go about our daily lives, we can trust that the Holy Spirit will connect us with those with open and fertile hearts. Introducing one person to the living Christ often opens an entire network of new connections and relationships.

THE MISSION FIELD WE ALL LIVE IN

Every Christ follower lives in a mission field of families, neighbors, co-workers or fellow students, friends, and those in our normal traffic patterns. Every individual we encounter also has a network of relationships made up of families, neighbors, co-workers, friends, and others. Being aware of the Kingdom principles of the mustard seed and yeast can help us realize our potential for the Kingdom by sharing the Gospel with one person. We can focus on one or a few to impact the many. It's also valuable to know what it means to be salt and light and realize that we can reproduce and multiply spiritual movements.

Every member of the Body of Christ has the capacity and opportunity to participate in growing the Kingdom of God.

In our orality training and practices with Living Water International over the past decade, we've observed that God often uses the most unlikely people to spread the Good News of Jesus. Sometimes all it takes is a spark that ignites a movement of reproducing communities of disciples and Churches. A mission leader in Zimbabwe participated in Living Water's Orality Training for Trainers. Over the following two years, he trained four thousand other pastors. According to reports from the Evangelical Fellowship of Zimbabwe, those 4,000 pastors had trained more than four hundred thousand others.

My longtime friend, Dick Eastman, recently spoke to a group at the Jericho Center in Colorado Springs on spiritual awakenings. He pointed out that every major movement of God throughout history started with a few praying people. He noted from research by scholar, author, and historian J. Edwin Orr that on average, these awakenings started on average with eleven praying people throughout Church history. As we pray according to the will of God, we can fully expect His power and blessing to follow.

SOWING AND REAPING

It was encouraging to recently reconnect with a man that I led to the Lord more than twenty-five years ago. He shared about several family members and co-workers with whom he had also come to the Lord. We seldom know how God may work in the lives of those we share with. If we are faithfully sowing the seed of God's Word into the lives of others, we can have confidence that, in some cases, it will take root and produce much fruit. When we sow abundantly, we can expect to reap an abundant harvest.

Some friends and I engaged a young man in conversation in an apartment complex. We were part of a ministry outreach where we intentionally shared the Gospel. As we chatted with the man, it was obvious that he was interested and open to the Lord. So, we invited him to have prayer with us, and he called on the Lord to forgive him and come into his life. About six other people in a cluster in a stairwell in the apartment complex overheard our conversation and prayer. We were surprised that six other people verbally joined and trusted the Lord when we started praying. When the Holy Spirit is at work, it always pays to expect the unexpected.

Reflecting on the many ways I've experienced God working in my life, I often think of one of my favorite Scripture passages, found in I Corinthians 1. In that Chapter, we are reminded that the foolishness of God is wiser than the wisdom of the world. We are told that God has not chosen many wise or influential by the world's standards. He has chosen the weak and lowly, which should encourage each of whom may not feel qualified. I have often told people that I grew up with an inferiority complex. Then later discovered that it wasn't a complex at all. That I was just inferior. However, we are all inferior in that all have sinned and fallen short of the glory of God. The good news is that the superior one, Christ Himself, is prepared to come into our lives and make us new creations.

The Lord Jesus makes us complete and gives us all things that pertain to life and godliness. He compensates for all our flaws and weaknesses. In fact, in our weakness His strength is made perfect and manifested through us. That was such a liberating experience years ago that made a major difference in my life and a multitude of others. These simple but profound Kingdom principles give us grace and enabling to live godly lives and be faithful witnesses and disciple-makers.

When we consider what the Kingdom of God is like, we need to consider all that the Lord has said about His Kingdom. In our Lord's model prayer, He refers to His Kingdom coming here on earth as it is in heaven. Jesus' prayer to His Father was, "Your Kingdom come, your will be done, on Earth as it is in heaven." So, wherever His will is being done is where His Kingdom is coming. We are also told in Scripture that the Kingdom of God is within us. As we acknowledge and submit to the Lordship and Kingship of Jesus is where the Kingdom is reigning. We reign in life through the Lord Jesus.

THE SIMPLICITY OF LIFE IN UNION WITH CHRIST

Years ago, Dr. Richard Halverson, United States Senate Chaplain, said, "Christianity started out in the region of Palestine (also known as the Land of Israel) with a relationship with a person, the Lord Jesus. Then it went to Greece and became a philosophy, went to Rome, and became an institution, then on to Europe and became a culture, and then came to America and became an enterprise." He emphasized the need to return to the simplicity of a relationship with the person of Jesus. That, of course, is happening in many ways, primarily among the oral cultures of the Global South. We in the Western World can learn so much from those places and movements. It is more evident in places with fewer trappings of modern religious traditions.

Many productive conversations are taking place these days regarding what it will take to complete the Great Commission. Which, in essence, is to communicate the Gospel to every person and make disciples of all nations. As I have interacted with Christ's followers in various parts of the world over the years, I have realized how much our thinking is influenced by our culture and various Church traditions.

Sometimes our culture and environment influence our thinking more than the Word of God. It's helpful when we can see past our modern western customs and Church traditions and focus more on the essentials of our life in union with Christ and the clear teaching of Scripture. Over the past few hundred years, Church traditions have made the Gospel of Jesus and what it means to follow Him more complicated than it needs to be.

From the story of the "Woman at the Well" in John 4, we know that the water that Jesus gives will become within us a spring or fountain of water, springing up to eternal life. Regarding our response to the commands and promises of the Word of God, the Apostle Paul tells us that some sow, some water, and some reap the harvest, but God gives the increase. God, the Holy Spirit, is prepared to work in us to will and do according to His good pleasure.

It is a privilege to be a part of the transformation of lives everywhere when we share the Living Water and the Living Word of the Lord Jesus with others. It is important to remember that we don't have to depend upon our human resources, speaking ability, or persuasive skills but are instruments of the Holy Spirit. We don't have to be great storytellers because we have great stories to tell. It is the Holy Spirit at work as we share the stories of Jesus and the Word of God who touches hearts and transforms lives.

God is an equal opportunity employer. He is willing to use all of us who make ourselves available to Him. He has equipped us with His indwelling life and desires to work in and through each of us to reveal Christ and advance His Kingdom. Throughout Scripture, we can observe how often certain themes show up repeatedly. Certainly, God thought repetition is important and how humans are prone to forget. We need constant reminders.

ANSWERS TO PRAYER

It is exciting to have a part in bringing new life to people by helping communities acquire access to clean water. What is even more exciting, however, is seeing people come to the Lord and become followers of Jesus. A woman I had the opportunity of leading to Christ a few years ago said, "Why didn't you come sooner? I wish I had done this many years ago." And, when people in a community get a new water well and clean water for the first time, they often say something like, we have been praying for water, wish you had come sooner. Many still lack access to clean water, but encouraging progress is being made.

In some parts of the world, people identified as Christians are denied access to the community water source. Living Water International partners with churches and other mission organizations in those regions to drill water wells and help with sanitation services and health and hygiene education. Then the believers freely share their clean, safe water with those who had previously denied them access to the community water supply. As a result, people often ask, "Why are you doing this?" The congregation's generosity removes the barriers and builds bridges for the message of Jesus.

Significant inroads are being made to reach the least and last unreached people groups. Clean water solutions are often the key that opens doors and builds bridges to people who need to hear and know about Jesus. When the thirsty come to Jesus and believe in Him, He said that out of our hearts will flow rivers of Living Water, according to John 7. The reproducing life of the Lord Jesus, in and through each of His followers, is bringing transformation and expanding the Kingdom of God.

CONCLUSION

As followers of Jesus, each of us should be encouraged to know that the Kingdom of God is coming wherever His will is being done here on earth as it is in heaven. (See Matthew 6: 9 -10) It is amazing that God has chosen to use ordinary people who trust and obey Him to advance His Kingdom. There is a future aspect to the Kingdom and a present-tense reality. Scripture also tells us that the Kingdom of God is within us. Years ago, there was a Kingdom and the dominion theology movement emerged. While there was some out-of-balance teaching in it, there is an aspect of the Kingdom Now living, and we do have a mandate to have dominion over the whole of creation, according to Genesis 1. When Jesus reigns as king in our lives, we are experiencing the Kingdom of God.

Chapter 11

How to Become a
Creative Genius

THE GENIUS IN US ALL

Creativity is a very important part of communicating the Gospel and making disciples. The best way of becoming a creative genius is by recognizing that, as believers in Christ, we are indwelt by deity. We have a creative genius, the Holy Spirit of God, living inside us. The genius of our union with Christ is that the creator, God of the universe, is living in us, and He is prepared to express His creativity through us. We can become co-creators with Him. It is a revolutionary idea that God's unlimited and creative power is available to us to the degree that we make ourselves available to Him.

Arts and orality have become important topics of discussion in recent years among Church and mission leaders. Understanding worldview and cultural value systems is vital to effectively make disciples in the global context. However, they are becoming increasingly important everywhere, even in North America and the modern Western world. Being flexible, adaptable, and open to change will help us in every area of life. Walking by faith and trusting God to give us His creative and innovative methods and strategies will enable us to recognize and seize ministry opportunities we might otherwise miss.

Over about five years, Living Water International, partnered with local Churches and conducted orality training with more than twelve hundred pastors, evangelists, missionaries, and Church planters in Ethiopia. On return trips, we hear amazing stories and testimonies of how God used the orality methods and strategies and how they are impacting and being reproduced.

PRAYER AND THE WORK OF THE SPIRIT

One man shared how they used to go into Muslim villages, pass out Gospel literature, and preach, and the people wanted to run them out of the community. After receiving the orality training, he said they tell stories, ask questions, have discussions, and build rapport, and the people wanted to follow Jesus! Of course, prayer and trusting the Holy Spirit for His creative methods are vital.

During one of our follow-up orality training for trainers sessions, an evangelist who had participated in previous training gave me the picture and told me a story. He had been reaching out to a Muslim community and told the Bible stories he had learned in the training. After telling some of the stories and engaging in conversations, the village chief, a Muslim imam, asked a question. He said, "Can Issa (Jesus) still do miracles today?" The evangelist said, "Yes, He can." The village chief then explained that his ten-year-old daughter had gone missing for several days. In desperation, the chief said if Issa could help find his daughter, he would become a follower of His.

The evangelist prayed with the chief and his family and called on the Lord to help find the daughter. The next day they found the daughter. As a result, the chief embraced the Gospel and confessed to Christ. Not only that, but his whole family also came to the Lord. Over time, the entire community embraced the Gospel and was transformed by becoming followers of Jesus.

POWER OF WATER AND THE WORD

Since the founding of Living Water International in 1990, we've heard numerous stories of communities being transformed. The "transforming power of water and the Word" has been a resounding theme over the years, and there is no one formula or recipe for God's activity. He is creative and unlimited in how He does it, and in many cases, we are amazed and surprised at His wondrous works. The most amazing thing, however, is that we, as His followers, can participate with Him. Out of our innermost being will flow rivers of Living Water, Jesus said, recorded in John 7.

At a meeting in Nairobi, Kenya a man approached me and said, "You changed my life." Of course, he was talking about Living Water as an organization. He told me how, Living Water International drilled a new water well in his village when he was a little boy. That well brought lifesaving clean water to a very needy community. Clean water, hygiene training, and sanitation services have brought new life and hope to the entire region. However, the spiritual transformation, the Living Water of Jesus, had the most long-lasting impact.

One of my mentors emphasized that the normal Christian life should be about the reproducing life of the Lord Jesus, in and through the redeemed humanity of every forgiven sinner. An important lesson in the orality movement is the power of simplicity and reproducibility. It's about getting back to how the Gospel spread so rapidly in the Early Church and how it's spreading now in the more communal, relational, oral cultures. The Holy Spirit uses ordinary, simple people who hear, respond, and share the Word of God. His Word is powerful to save and transform lives. The message is more important than the messenger, and each of us can participate in expanding His Kingdom by telling our story and His story.

Sometimes people hear these remarkable stories of what God is doing around the world and think 'that could never happen here or with me.' That reminds me of a quote from A. W. Tozer when he said,

> "Anything God has ever done at any time; He can do now. Anything He has ever done anywhere; He can do here. And anything He has ever done through anyone; He can do through you."[3]

That should certainly be an encouragement to all of us who are followers of Jesus. We are all indwelt by His life, temples of the Holy Spirit, equipped and enabled for His divine presence and power. God has made us new creations in Christ, able ministers of the new covenant and ministers of reconciliation. Reflecting on these truths should give us a passion for sharing our life in Christ with others.

When we think of how God has worked throughout history, often all it takes is something as simple as a story or a conversation that transforms life. A transformed life can transform other lives, even families and communities. The good news is that we don't have to wait for some sweeping movement of God. He is the same yesterday, today, and forever. His provision for the fullness of life in Christ is available to all who come to and believe in Him. In fact, He says that if we do so, rivers of Living Water will flow out of our hearts (our innermost being). He was speaking of the Holy Spirit and His divine activity.

---

3 A. W. Tozer, Leadership weekly, 10/9/02

OUTPOURING OF THE SPIRIT BRINGS CREATIVE EXPRESSIONS

Many of those who lived through and experienced the Asbury Revival and Jesus Revolution of the late 1960s and early 1970s are seeing many parallels with what is going on in the world today. These kinds of spiritual movements usually foster several new creative and innovative witness and ministry efforts. More people are praying for revival and spiritual awakening now than at any other time in history. More people are also seeking answers, solutions, and being open to the Lord more than ever. The prophet Joel spoke of a time when the Lord poured out His Spirit on all humanity.

A woman in Honduras who attended an orality training workshop was legally blind. She learned the story of Bartimaeus, the blind beggar. The evening after the first training day, the woman was at home reflecting on the story. She closed her eyes and said, "Lord, I believe! Lord, I believe!" When she opened her eyes, she said she could see. The next morning on the second training day, the woman shared her experience with the group. There was much rejoicing for everyone to realize that Jesus can still give sight to the blind today, both physically and spiritually.

When we consider the background, context, and account in Scripture of the healing of the blind beggar Bartimaeus, we see that it contains many lessons. This takes place toward the latter part of Jesus' ministry and life on earth. He often taught His disciples important lessons while traveling on the road. Jesus talked to the disciples about the importance of having a servant's heart and attitude. He gave them principles of servant leadership. In fact, He told them that the son of man came not to be served but to serve others. He taught them that if one wants to be great in God's Kingdom, he must learn to be the servant of all.

After learning this story, trainees are asked such questions as,

- What do we learn about the people's attitude toward this blind beggar?
- Why were the people trying to keep this man away from Jesus?
- What can we learn about who Jesus values and has time for?
- What do we learn from the fact that the blind beggar Bartimaeus threw off his coat to come to Jesus?
- How did this blind man know to call out to Jesus?
- What do we learn about prayer and being specific and persistent?
- How did the people's attitudes change after Jesus told them to call the man to him?

This short story has many lessons and applications about faith, prayer, and being persistent and specific in our requests of God. In our orality training, we point out that this blind beggar, Bartimaeus, could have been blind from birth. He obviously was an oral learner. Someone must have told him stories about Jesus, the son of David. He had heard enough to exercise faith in calling on the Lord.

We point out that there are many spiritually blind people in the world today. We ask, what do spiritually blind people need? Obviously, they need spiritual eyesight. Jesus said, "Unless a person is born again, he or she cannot see the Kingdom of God. We can compare this with the story of the blind beggar, that we need spiritual eyesight to be born of the Spirit to follow Jesus. Also, when people are truly born again, the result is that they have a new heart and a new desire to follow and please the Lord. Many people try to follow Jesus without being born again.

SPIRITUAL APPLICATIONS

In many countries where Living Water International works, beggars and blind people are much more common than in the Western world. These people can relate to the context of the story and make applications to their own lives. They discover many profound insights. Additional questions for discussion might be:

- What do we learn from the fact that after the blind man received his sight, he started following Jesus?
- Is there a lesson in this for us? Is there a spiritual lesson and application?
- What do spiritually blind people need?
- What do people do when they are born again, born of the Spirit, and receive their spiritual eyesight?
- People often conclude that one must receive spiritual sight to truly follow Jesus.

Orality training participants can spend hours discussing short, simple stories when the right questions are asked. The questions about the stories are usually from the following three categories: What do we observe from the story? What does it mean? And how does it apply to our lives? People are always amazed at how much they can learn from simple stories.

Focusing on learning a little, practicing a lot, implementing immediately, and telling the stories has a powerful impact. People respond well to the emphasis on learning only a few stories but learning a few stories that they tell many people well. Oral cultures learn in the community, so they benefit from the collective memory of the group. When people learn stories well and discuss them often, they tend to tell them to others, and the message is spread quickly. Repetition, reproducibility, and multiplication are important factors in the orality movement.

A NEW AND CREATIVE METHOD

Once pastors, evangelists, missionaries, and Church planters gain a better understanding of the ancient methods of orality, they are energized with new visions and passion. A pastor in South Asia told of how he had been using biblical storytelling to present the Gospel for many years. After participating in Living Water's Orality Training, he shared that reproducibility had been missing in his previous approach. He recognized that with more repetition and engagement, it was more reproducible. He said, "From now on, I'll use this method." A pastor in Central America said, "Now I see that with this method, I can equip, train and mobilize storytelling evangelists at every level of age and education."

According to my friend Mark Snowden, oral learners and oral cultures are probably the least evangelized group in the nation[4]. He says that if we are serious about reaching the people of this generation who have yet to be believers, we must understand how they communicate and learn and develop skills for bringing the message to them. It is estimated that over 90 percent of all preachers of the Gospel have been trained to communicate only to literates using an analytical format, which oral learners find nearly impossible to relate to or remember. Outlines, steps, principles, lists, and similar constructions assume literacy. Within oral cultures, people do not learn and retain their understanding of truth and life in these ways.

---

4 Mark Snowden, *Orality: The Next Wave of Mission Advance*, International Journal of Frontier Missions, Jan-Feb 04

In addition to the primary oral learners, mainly in the more undeveloped parts of the world, there are many oral preference learners. Many well-educated and highly literate people are still oral-preference learners and communicators. A friend who is president of one of the largest ministries in the world says he is an oral preference learner. He has advanced degrees from a leading university but still prefers to communicate and learn orally. When we think of simple and relational methods of witnessing and ministering to others, it helps to think outside the box. In other words, various mental models and creative methods open all kinds of possibilities. Think of the tools of the age, modern technology, and the tools of the ages. Tools of the ages would be word of mouth, narrative or storytelling, and other oral art forms.

CONCLUSION

Creativity and innovation have become increasingly valued in today's world. It is important to recognize that God is the originator of creativity, and we can be co-creators with the Creator God of the universe. These truths can apply to communicating the Gospel and making disciples. The Holy Spirit's unlimited and creative redemptive activities can be released through the least of His children. It's been a great encouragement for me to continually remind myself that I have a creative genius living inside of me. That is true of each of us who are born of the Spirit.

Chapter 12

Why it is Imperative to See from God's Perspective

A NEED FOR 50/20 VISION

A long-time friend and mentor used to talk about the need for having a 50/20 Vision. It's based on Genesis 50:20 when Joseph said to his brothers, after being abused by them, "You planned evil against me, but God meant it for good." There are many examples throughout history where God intervenes in human experience to bring good out of bad situations. However, the realization of that truth can best be experienced when we see things from God's perspective, seeing past the seen and temporal to the unseen and eternal.

Another mentor of mine used to emphasize that every negative has a positive. Furthermore, the more negative the negative, the more positive the positive. So, when life's circumstances seem really bad, we can look to the Lord and expect Him to intervene and use what is going on to bring good from it. We often observe how God shows up in the most difficult times and the darkest places. It's not always easy to remember these important spiritual truths. That's why repetition is so vital to our spiritual journey, and it is also the mother of all learning.

GOD WORKS IN CRISIS

It's important to remember that when things really get bad, we can look to the Lord and trust He will show Himself strength on our behalf. History is filled with examples of how God used those crises difficult experiences for His divine purposes. However, focusing on the inward and eternal is important, rather than the outward and temporary.

I enlisted in the Air Force right after High School. As I left home for basic training, my Daddy told me, "Remember that all things work together for good to those who love the Lord." He shared that his dad had told him the same thing when he was leaving for the Army during World War II. I later encountered some difficulties and wondered, "Where is that verse in the Bible." (I was not so knowledgeable of the Bible at the time). Of course, I discovered it was Romans 8:28. Over the years, the Lord has brought that verse to my mind many times.

More than forty years ago, I heard a Bible teacher on the radio talking about the purpose of difficulties, suffering, and problems in our lives. He talked about how God uses those experiences to:

1. Focus our faith
2. Fashion our character
3. Fit us for service

It is remarkable how a phrase, a statement, a quote, or a story can stick in our minds and change our lives. It's a reminder that the Holy Spirit will bring to our memory what we have heard or read of His Word. It illustrates the power of a word or message and how we should be aware and intentional about what we say and how it can impact people's lives.

It is liberating to realize that God is working all things after the counsel of His own will. The Lord can use all our negative and positive experiences for His purposes. It's our perspective, our 50/20 Vision, which allows us to be fruitful and make an impact for His Kingdom's purposes. Keeping our focus on the Lord enables us to endure hardships and difficulties. Having God's perspective helps us to recognize His redemptive activities and those divine appointments for witness and ministry. Opportunities we might miss otherwise. Those opportunities may present themselves during a routine visit to a medical center, an auto repair business, or a shopping trip. They can also come in times of serious crises or disasters.

Hard times come to everyone. When we face hard times, we can ask the Lord, "How do you want me to respond? What are you up to, and how do you want to use me in this situation?" God will often use us in those times to demonstrate His character to those around us. Then the door can open to share and make known the hope within us, Christ Himself. Someone has said that when bad times come, character is revealed.

An automobile accident, a medical emergency, a crisis situation, or even a global pandemic can result in meeting new people, forming new relationships, and discovering new ministry opportunities. Those occasions can often result in spiritual light shining into new places. As ambassadors of Christ, we expect the Lord to orchestrate our lives and circumstances to accomplish His purposes. Living out of an awareness of these truths can help us recognize witness and ministry opportunities that we might otherwise miss.

UNUSUAL WITNESS OPPORTUNITIES

Two ministry colleagues and I were returning to the United States from several days in Liberia, where we had been conducting orality training for pastors and Church leaders. We had about a four-hour layover in Brussels, Belgium. Our plane landed at about 5:00 a.m. in Brussels on March 22, 2016. We cleared the border and security checkpoints, which took longer than normal as security was very tight that day. After finally clearing, we relaxed at a coffee shop since we still had a couple of hours before our flight was scheduled to depart for the United States.

Around 8:00 a.m., we heard a loud explosion, and major chaos broke out. It was a Muslim terrorist suicide bombing near the check-in area of the airport. The chaos continued for several hours as the airport terminals were evacuated. We were taken out on the tarmac, loaded on buses, and taken to hangers and other safe facilities.

It was a cold day, and a single vent was putting out warm air in the hangar so about forty people were huddled around it. I said to Rob, one of our travel companions, "This reminds me of that story from the Bible about Jesus calming the storm." I went on to tell the story to Rob, but the forty or so people there could hear it. We talked about how Jesus can still bring calmness today in our storms of life. That also opened the way for other conversations and sharing the Gospel with this very captive audience.

The four-hour layover that turned into a five-day delay provided a good number of incredible witness and ministry opportunities. We rented a car and drove to Amsterdam to catch flights back to the States. When we see things from God's perspective, we can more easily recognize the opportunity of being salt and light in any situation.

He can use the most painful and negative experiences to His glory and our good. In times of crisis, people are often more open to engaging in spiritual conversations and receiving prayer. People will notice if you have calmness during a storm or difficult time.

The Brussels Terrorist bombing received widespread international news coverage. At the airports and on the planes returning home, I had several opportunities to share my experience. Many of those conversations turned into witness opportunities as well. I was able to bring the Lord into many of those conversations and share how we saw the hand of God during the disaster. On my trans-Atlantic flight, several flight attendants were interested in hearing more about my experience in Brussels. In fact, they were so moved that they prepared me a special food tray as a gift.

Praying and asking the Lord to give us ears to hear and eyes to see what He is doing in any given situation can make a difference. Of course, we know that God delights in answering our prayers when we are praying according to His will. He also tells us that if we lack wisdom, we should ask Him, and He will give it to us. The important thing is to believe and expect the Lord to answer those prayers. Prayer in this way causes us to be more alert and attentive to the circumstances and people around us. Then when we test the water, so to speak, we'll more likely recognize God's hand and can respond accordingly.

REAL-LIFE LESSONS

A couple of young men who had heard me speak on personal evangelism requested an opportunity to go out with me to share the Gospel. I have made that offer many times, and some have taken the challenge. This time another more mature brother was available and joined us for an afternoon of mingling with people at a busy shopping mall. Sometimes all together, and part of the time, we split up to reach out to shoppers and others in the mall. We showed ourselves friendly, greeted people, and asked a few general and non-threatening questions. Following are a few of the questions and approaches we used:

- Have you noticed any signs of spiritual awakening in this area?
- Have you noticed how many people are becoming more aware of their need for the Lord?
- Would you be interested in knowing how you can have a more personal and intimate relationship with God?
- Have you been thinking more about the Lord lately?
- Do you have an interest in spiritual matters?
- Has the Lord been good to you today?
- Has anyone talked with you about the Lord this week?

Any number of variations of these questions can be instrumental in beginning a Jesus-focused conversation. It usually works better if these questions come after a pleasant greeting and showing interest in the person. Over about three hours that Sunday afternoon, twenty-eight people were open for spiritual conversations and prayed to receive Christ. It is important to recognize only some who pray and confess faith in Christ have a born-again experience. However, it is also important to be aware that when we can pray and present the Gospel, the Holy Spirit transforms lives.

I learned from Bill Bright, founder of Campus Crusade for Christ (now Cru) years ago, that our role as believers is to "Share Christ in the power of the Holy Spirit and leave the results to God." That may be a little simplistic. However, it is liberating to know that we can't change lives, but it is the Gospel that is the power of God unto salvation for everyone who believes. We get to deliver the message. We get to be good news reporters. Of course, the Scripture tells us we are ambassadors of Christ, ministers of reconciliation, and able ministers of the New Covenant. We can have confidence that God will work as we step out and act in faith in His Word. It is not our ability or presentation skills but the power of the Spirit who touches hearts and changes lives.

Over the years, it has been a real privilege to attend many conventions, conferences, and other meetings. Usually, on the second day of the meetings, I ask questions of those who serve and support the gathering. That normally includes security guards, janitorial staff, maid service, and wait staff. I ask, "Has anyone talked with you about the Lord this week?" Most will say no. However, whatever the answer, that approach often leads to a spiritual conversation and opportunity to share the Lord. That simple approach has led to a large number of people coming to the Lord.

At a major convention in Washington, D.C., several years ago, a colleague and I had the opportunity to lead more than twenty people to confess their faith in Christ. These were mostly employees or staff at the convention center hotel. At the end of the convention, we were able to get a few of them together for a time of prayer. The idea was to create a plan to stay in touch and encourage each other in their new life in Christ. In a sense, I suppose you could call that a Church planting effort. Many Churches have gotten started in these ways.

CONCLUSION

Unless a person is born again, he or she cannot **see** the Kingdom of God. We cannot have God's perspective without spiritual eyesight, which comes with spiritual union with Christ. The miracle of the new birth gives us the capacity to see from God's perspective. The natural, unregenerate person cannot receive or perceive God's things because they are spiritually discerned. Actually, spiritual truth is communicated to the human spirit by the Holy Spirit. The beauty of our relationship with Jesus is that we can count on God's leading and guiding us into all truth. That faith/trust relationship gives us the ability to see from God's perspective.

Chapter 13

What it Takes to Live a Godly Life and Be a Faithful Witness

A FRUITFUL METHOD

Years ago, it was a joyous and liberating discovery when I realized that God didn't expect me to produce or perform on my own. After a few years of trying and working hard to be a good Christian and a faithful witness, I discovered I didn't have what it takes. However, with that discovery, I also realized that Christ in me was the key. In Revelation 1:5, reference is made to Jesus Christ as the faithful witness. In reality, He is the only true faithful witness. The beauty of our relationship with Him is that He is prepared to be and do through us what we can never do with our human strength and resources. Following that spiritual transformation, I began seeing more people come to Christ, just accidentally, than I was able to produce before on purpose.

It was the difference in my trying to do something for God, rather than trusting and letting Him work through me. It is clear from Scripture that the just shall live by faith and without faith it is impossible to please God. Faith is foundational to a godly life and a fruitful and faithful witness.

In the mid-1980s, in Washington D.C., I got to know a man named Herb who was head of a major federal government agency. The friend who introduced us told me that Herb had one of the most fruitful and effective ministries of anyone in the city at that time. He led several weekly Bible studies with military officers in the Pentagon, White House staff, media executives, and other senior government officials. He was known to have led several people to Christ almost on a weekly basis. One of his favorite methods of communicating the Gospel and sharing spiritual truth was to talk about strawberries.

Historically, strawberries have symbolized spring, rebirth, righteousness, and love. While strawberries are a familiar fruit, several possible meanings are attributed to them. Some have suggested that the strawberry represents rebirth since they are the first to ripen in spring and represent good health. In some traditions, strawberries represent the good fruits of the righteous, friendship, and love. Even in medieval art, the strawberry plant is a prominent image.

By the 1300s, it was common to find strawberries pictured in Italian, Flemish, and German art and in English miniatures as a symbol of perfect righteousness. It was believed that the strawberry was a cure for depressive illnesses and that its presence suggested the healing powers of Christ that lead us to eternal salvation. Its three-partitioned leaf reminds some of the Holy Trinity. Even more remarkable, some see drops of the blood of Christ as the fruit points downward. The five petals of its white flower bring to mind His five wounds.

BEING WHAT WE HAVE BECOME

It's been my experience that many Christ-followers do not see themselves as righteous or complete in Christ. Therefore, they feel they need to strive for perfection. That often results in trying to become what we think we should be rather than being what we have already become in Christ. However, it is liberating to come to that place of accepting our acceptance, accepting ourselves as God has accepted us in Christ. Of course, it's the finished work of Christ on the cross that makes that all possible. Fruitful, victorious, and righteous living is not about self-improvement but Christ's replacement. It's the Galatians 2:20 reality that I no longer live, but Christ is living in me. It's good to remember also, from the rest of that verse, that the life we now live, we live by the faith of and in the Son of God. Being a faithful witness will then become more of a spontaneous expression of His life in and through us.

It was a major turning point in my life when I came to an awareness of the futility of self-effort. Then, I could enter and appropriate the fullness of life in union with Christ. There was a new freedom and joy in sharing that liberating message with others. I began to see more people come to Christ after making that discovery and realization. ,. Again, It was the difference between God at work through me rather than my activities on His behalf. Just like we can't save ourselves, we can't live a fruitful, righteous life apart from Him. As we have received Christ Jesus the Lord, we are to walk in Him, as we are told in Scripture.

There is a great need today among followers of Jesus to discover more fully, who we are in Christ, who He is in us, and how to relate to Him. We all have equal access to the throne of grace and can come to Him at any time and find rest in our souls. Resting in Christ does not mean inactivity but ceasing from our own activity and appropriating His unlimited love and power. It's about the reproducing life of the Lord Jesus, in and through each of us who trust and obey Him. That outworking of the indwelling Christ will result in godly lives and being faithful witnesses.

The most important thing about anything is its purpose. When we think about our purpose here on earth, looking back to the beginning of creation in the book of Genesis is helpful. Chapter one, verse twenty-six, tells us we were created in the image and likeness of God. That is, we are to be a physical, visible expression of the invisible character of God. Of course, because of the fall, the image of God was marred in humanity. The good news is that the Lord Jesus came into the world, lived a perfect life, and demonstrated what true humanity was to be and do. It was the life that He lived that qualified Him for the death that He died. Furthermore, the death that He died qualifies us for the life that He gives and lives in us. It's faith that converts that truth into reality.

When we grasp the significance of the creation of mankind, we can better understand the implications of salvation, which is a re-creation. Because of the finished work of Christ on the cross, we can be made new creations and restored to true humanity. That is the life of God in the soul of mankind that produces the likeness of God in our character. The greater awareness we have of these truths, the more we can rest in the reality of who we are in Christ and who He is living in us. The Apostle Paul reminds us that for us to live is Christ living in us.

WITNESS IN WORD AND DEED

Helping people understand the overall purposes of God is important in realizing how we are to live our lives now. That is, living in harmony with the will and purposes of our Creator. It's not just about forgiveness of sins and heaven someday, but also about Christ now living in us and communicating His life through us. What people see in us is sometimes more important than what we say. However, both are vital when it comes to being faithful witnesses. We are to be witnesses in word and deed, demonstration and proclamation. Of course, the proclamation part can take on many forms of expression. Hopefully, by the many stories and examples in this book, one will understand the variety of ways His life can be lived out through us.

While sharing the Gospel and discussing salvation with others, relative to their knowledge of eternal life, I have often heard people say something like, "I hope so; I'm doing the best I can." Many are unsure of their salvation because they think of their own works or goodness. Of course, we all come short of the glory of God. Some may have a good understanding of the fact that we are saved by grace through faith. However, they may still have a works maintenance mentality. Jesus said, "I am the way, the truth, and the life." He is the truth about the way, in that He is the only way we can become a Christian. He is also the truth about the life, in that He is the only way for us to be the Christian we have become.

These concepts seem to some like a play on words, but for many they can be life changing. The fact that Jesus is the truth about God and the truth about man that is man as He as God intended man to be. In this context, we're talking about mankind, including women, men, and children. In our contemporary culture, humanity is a more acceptable term. In his books, *The Saving Life of Christ*, and *The Mystery of Godliness*, Major Ian Thomas illustrates these truths with great clarity.

NOT SELF-IMPROVEMENT, BUT CHRIST REPLACEMENT

Another one of my mentors from years ago was author and missionary statesman Norman Grubb. Among the many books that he wrote was a small book titled, *The Key to Everything*. In that book, he talks about us being containers of deities. He points out that the most important thing about a container is its content. Another way of thinking about these truths is that God is not so interested in our self-improvement as He is in Christ's replacement. Not I, but Christ is the heart of the matter when it comes to godly living and being a faithful witness. It's out of the heart the mouth speaks. So, when our heart is right with the Lord, we can expect to be a more spontaneous witness.

One of the things that I've noticed over the decades of witnessing and sharing the Gospel is that when people have a genuine encounter with the living Christ, there is a desire to share Him with others. Motivation is more important than education, personality, or abilities. Having spent many years in higher education, I've observed that some of the most educated people are sometimes the least fruitful in their spiritual life. On the other hand, I've known many godly men and women with little formal education who have had amazingly fruitful and productive lives and ministries.

As an orality practitioner and trainer for many years, I've seen how simple and common people come alive with a great passion for sharing the Lord. Many times, it's simply learning a few stories from Scripture well enough to retell and pass on. An important aspect is to focus on the essentials. Many secondary issues can distract from what the main message should be. That is Christ and Him crucified, keeping the focus on Jesus, who He is, and what He has done on our behalf.

A NARRATIVE THEOLOGY OF THE MOST IMPORTANT TRUTHS

One of the great joys of traveling and working in various parts of the world is learning about common social and cultural issues. Relative to the Great Commission of communicating the Gospel and making disciples, a few essentials need to be top of mind. Consider how much and what people need to know to begin a relationship with the Lord. Then, how much and what do they need to know to become a reproducing follower of Jesus. In our experience with Living Water

International and partner Churches and organizations, we've gained some important lessons. Following are some topics that have given us a framework for discipling new converts anywhere on the planet:

- Who He is (the character of God)
- Who we are (the nature of humanity)
- Why we are (the purpose of God)
- What we have (the provision of God to carry out His purpose)
- How we live (practical principles of the outworking of the in-dwelling Christ)

Everything in the Bible can be related to one or more of these topics. With a set of stories from the Gospels, with the appropriate pre- and post-story questions, discussion, and dialogue, we give a community, a village, or a tribal group a simple narrative theology. Our focus is on the essentials necessary to begin a relationship with the Lord and to become a reproducing follower of Jesus.

Burkina Faso is a country in West Africa that is primarily an oral culture. Several years ago, a colleague and I conducted Bible storying and orality training with more than 1,000 people. At that time, the language group in that region had no Scripture translated into their language. Furthermore, 85 percent of the country is considered illiterate. However, we prefer to define people based something other than what they can't do, like reading or writing. Rather we like to focus on what they can do; they are oral learners. In many places where we work and conduct trainings, the people may speak eight or ten languages. They may not read or write any of them. They are often very bright and intelligent but learn, communicate, and process information differently from the more literate and print-based cultures.

A couple of years after conducting the initial orality training in Burkina Faso, we returned to do more advanced orality training for trainers.

In these training sessions, we discovered that fifteen of the participants were in the training from two years earlier. We heard several of them talk about how they had used the training and how many were coming to Christ. With a local missionary and an interpreter, we had a session with the fifteen and asked, as best they could remember, how many had come to Christ since that first training. Those fifteen had counted 785 who responded to the Gospel since the initial training sessions. We can only imagine how many more have been impacted by the other 900 plus who received the same training.

When these impact stories are communicated to Church and ministry leaders in North America, there seems to be a growing awareness and interest with many to know more. The basic principles of storytelling and oral methods are universal in their applications. A key factor is getting back to the basics of how most people, have learned and communicated vital information over the longest period of time. We continuously emphasize that these are the ancient ways Jesus shared truth, instructed his followers, and made reproducing disciple-makers.

CONCLUSION

In Revelation 1:5, as was mentioned earlier and is worth mentioning again, that Jesus Christ is referred to as The Faithful Witness. He is the only true witness, and with His indwelling presence and divine enabling, He can make us become faithful witnesses. In like manner, only God can produce godly lives. The sooner we realize that we don't have what it takes to live godly lives and be faithful witnesses, the sooner we can appropriate His provision and let Him do in and through us what we can never do in our human resources. Jesus said, "My grace is sufficient for you, for My strength is made perfect in weakness." (II Cor. 12:9)

Chapter 14

How to Become an Effective Agent of Transformation

LESSONS FROM HISTORY

A few years ago, I had a conversation with a friend who is a biblical scholar and historian. He shared some conditions just before the First and Second Great Awakenings in the United States. Things were very bad. There was a lot of turbulence and disturbing developments. It is amazing when we observe the parallels between cultural issues and societal conditions between then and now. The moral and spiritual decline sets the stage for revival and spiritual awakening and increasing numbers of people coming to an awareness of their need for the Lord.

Whether they are defined as revivals, renewals, awakenings, or movements of God, we have been blessed to experience several in the history of this nation. Many more have happened throughout the rest of the world. It has been a great blessing to have personally benefited from several movements of God in my lifetime. The Asbury Revival and the Jesus movement of the early 1970's were among those. As a college student at the time, I experienced a spiritual transformation and began to actively share the Lord and see many come to Christ. A key factor for me was a new passion for sharing with others what God had done in my life. It was certainly a personal spiritual awakening for me that became contagious.

Many articles and books have been written, as well as sermons and lectures, giving accounts of how the Lord worked during that period. There has also been an ongoing ripple effect that still impacts today. Many believe that the turbulence of the 1960s set the stage for that movement. All the developments happening in the world today may be pointing toward a coming revival of some sort.

IMPACT ON THE ACADEMY

In 1995, God sparked revival and awakening on college, university, and seminary campuses. Beginning at Howard Payne University, as well as Houston Christian University, the move of the Spirit eventually spread to more than fifty campuses around the country. Several articles and books were written during that season, giving an account of how the Lord was a work. There was much brokenness, repentance, and open confession that were contagious. All such movements are certainly accelerating the spreading of the Gospel.

Over the past decade, there have been several encouraging spiritual movements through our orality training and Church mobilization strategies with Living Water International. We have received feedback where large numbers of people have come to Christ by telling Bible stories they learned at orality training events. Reports of disciple-making and Church planting movements have accelerated in areas where we have conducted the training. Ordinary followers of Jesus learn biblical stories, the skills of asking questions and then spread the Good News in the power of the Holy Spirit.

Upon a return trip to Haiti, one of the pastors who participated in an earlier orality training shared some of its impact. He shared that his Church was growing as a result of using the storytelling methods, but also, the training had enhanced their Church planting efforts. The Church in his region was growing and reproducing. He attributed it to the Bible storying and orality training workshops we conducted a couple of years before. Many of those in the training sessions were women and children who had received little or no formal education.

Increasing numbers of Church and mission leaders are sensing that we could be on the verge of the next Great Awakening. Renewals, revivals, and awakenings can take on many forms of expression and may look different from past movements. They can be personal or corporate. It is wonderful to be part of a corporate move of God. However, we do not have to wait for some sweeping motion of God. He is ready and prepared to renew each of us as we seek Him with our whole heart.

MOVING PAST MISCONCEPTIONS

A friend and I were at a medical center reception area and engaged in casual conversations with some family members and relatives of patients. We asked how their loved ones were doing and if we could pray for them. Those connections resulted in several fruitful conversations. Most people are open and eager to receive prayer, especially during sickness or need. It is amazing how those simple gestures can open new witness or ministry opportunities and sometimes create long-term relationships.

A misconception is assuming that people are closed or resistant to the Gospel. It is so easy to prejudge people based on outward appearance. Many people are much more open and receptive than we think. We sometimes have preconceived ideas about how people might respond if we make an effort. So, we don't even make the effort. It is normally easier not to say anything than it is to reach out and say something. Therefore, many opportunities are missed. Our most feeble efforts can sometimes have a life-changing impact, saving lives and changing people's eternal destinies.

A shopkeeper I engaged in conversation at a mall told me he had been in this country fifteen years. He immigrated from what we often refer to as a creative access country, where there are few Churches and a very low percentage of Christians. I could have assumed that surely, in those fifteen years, someone would have shared the Gospel with him. That, of course, was a false assumption. He said that no one had ever told him about Jesus. He was very open and eager to learn about what it means to know and follow Jesus.

With all the Churches, Bibles, the internet, Gospel radio, and television programs, there are still more than two billion people in the world today who are unreached. Many of those may be people we rub shoulders with every day. Sadly, studies have shown that more than 90 percent of professing Christians in the United States never share their faith or lead others to Christ. However, once someone observes how the Lord can use our witness and the power of the Gospel, it often ignites a passion to reach out and take a step of faith.

All that is going on in the world these days seems to be creating a greater awareness of the spiritual vacuum in many people's lives. It's causing many to think more about their need for the Lord. We hear reports that more people are turning to the Lord now than at any other time in history. Hopefully, followers of Jesus are beginning to see more opportunities to reach out with the love and message of Jesus. The prophet Joel spoke of a time when the Spirit of God would be poured out on all humanity. He said it is a time to put in the sickle because the harvest is ripe (Joel 3:13). In other words, seize the opportunities. Wherever we connect with people, virtually or personally, we can be salt and light to those around us and the world.

CONCLUSION

It is important to remember that the darkness is darkest before the dawn. God often does His greatest work in the darkest places and most difficult times. Historically, during those seasons of darkness and difficulty, God raises up ordinary individuals to become agents of change and transformation. Being an agent of transformation has often been where God shows Himself strong on our behalf and does what only He can do. God delights to work In ways that cannot be explained in terms of human resources or activities.

No one desires to be in dark places and difficult situations. However, when they come, we can turn our eyes upon Jesus, call upon Him, and trust Him to make us agents of transformation. I often remind myself of the words of the late Samuel Chadwick, "Inadequate men are always doing impossible things, and ordinary men achieve extraordinary results. God's biggest things seem to be done by the most unlikely people."

Chapter 15

Why Reproducibility is Vital to Advancing the Gospel

THE POWER OF ORAL LEARNING

While many, especially in the Global North are just now hearing about orality, it is, in fact, a significant breakthrough in Church and Mission movements. Some Church and Mission leaders acknowledge that more people are coming to faith in Christ through orality-based methods than text-based and literate methods. The case can be made that orality is changing the face of churches and missions around the world. The rapidly reproducing Church-planting and disciple-making movements are taking place primarily among oral cultures.

Those of us who have been involved as practitioners and trainers for any length of time are keenly aware of what an amazing learning journey we are on. It is encouraging to see pastors and other Church and Mission leaders come alive with new passion and vision when they experience orality methods and strategies firsthand. We often say that orality is better experienced than explained. One of its most compelling features is that people can see the power of demonstration, participation, and explanation. Instead of trying to take our literate-based, modern Western models to the rest of the world, we are recognizing that there is great value in what we are learning from more relational, communal, oral cultures.

Initially, some think of orality methods or storytelling as useful only for children's bedtime stories or in places where people can't read or do not have Scripture in their language. However, when we take a deeper look, we recognize the universal applications. For many years, the United Nations Educational, Scientific and Cultural Organization (UNESCO) reported that approximately eighty percent of the world's population was literate, and some mission agencies planned their strategies in light of those statistics. It is true that perhaps as many as eighty percent of the world can read something. However, a better question is, can they read, comprehend, and reproduce the message of Scripture?

The reproducibility aspects are what makes these concepts and principles so important. When we think of global movements, we need to acknowledge that we in North America are part of the globe. Oral preference learners and communicators are everywhere. While we don't want to limit our methods and strategies of communicating the gospel and making disciples to oral methods, it is the cutting edge to advancing our Lord's great commission. Again, it's vital to use all the ancient ways and modern methods for spreading the good news of Jesus.

THE BEGINNING OF A LEARNING JOURNEY

As a young boy growing up, I decided I wanted to become one of the world's leading experts on something. I just didn't know what. However, I wanted to make a difference in the world, and looking back, I believe God put that desire in my heart. Then, in 1983 I was introduced to the concepts of orality, oral cultures, and oral traditions. When I learned a little and discovered that so few people knew about this field of study, I thought, "I can become an expert in this field because there's such little competition." In subsequent years, I got acquainted with some leading scholars, researchers, and experts in orality and related disciplines. At that time, not many people were talking about orality or even familiar with the term, and very limited resources were available. So, I began asking questions, researching and communicating with people who seemed knowledgeable about orality and related topics. I began reading what I could find on the subject and developing some methods to train others.

During a visit to the U.S. Center for World Mission (now known as Frontier Ventures), I came across a book by Herbert V. Klem, *Oral Communication of the Scripture: Insights From African Oral Art*. It was initially a doctoral dissertation he published in 1982. The discovery of Herbert Klem's book and various other resources led me on an amazing learning journey, which I am still on. I found out later that his work was influential with many others who became leaders in the orality movement that emerged in later years. Dr. Grant Lovejoy, one of the leading scholars and practitioners in the orality movement, points out that "5.7 billion people in the world are oral communicators (because they are illiterate, or their reading comprehension is inadequate). In other words, they are oral learners by necessity or by preference. That number was based on research from 2012. So, the number could be much higher now.

We in the West can learn much from oral cultures. Many oral cultures have similar characteristics to those who lived during the times of Jesus and the early Church. They are still using the ancient ways of learning, communicating and processing information.

THE POWER OF SIMPLICITY

When we ask the right questions of Mission and Church leaders with a global and cross-cultural perspective, they usually come to the right conclusions. For example, we often ask questions like, "Who in all of world history is our best example of an effective communicator, trainer, and disciple-maker?" Of course, we recognize that Jesus is our best model and example. We might ask,

- How did Jesus communicate the Good News of God?
- How did He train and make disciples?
- Can we do it the way He did it?

Those questions lead us to consider the power of simplicity and re-producibility. Simplicity does not mean simplistic or shallow. In fact, orality methods can be used to communicate important theological themes and in-depth spiritual truths.

An important point we make in any context is that the same God who lived in Jesus Christ two thousand years ago is living in every believer who has been born of the Spirit. The same Holy Spirit is actively engaged in our lives and in the world today. That awareness gives people great confidence that we can enter into His redemptive activities, tell the good story (news), and expect His divine intervention. People with a heart for God and receive and act on His Word can experience God's grace, love, and power in remarkable ways.

With a growing awareness and interest in Orality, more people are realizing the multi-faceted aspects of the Orality movement. There are even streams inside streams. For example, the Bible Storying stream, Chronological Bible Storying, Thematic, Topical, Relational, and Panoramic Bible Storying. Living Water International basic Orality Training, uses Contextual Bible Storying. It is a blending and pollinating from several different streams within the movement. What makes this training so effective is the focus on learning a little, practicing a lot, implementing immediately, and telling the stories often. Simplicity and reproducibility are important factors as well.

MULTIFACETED ASPECTS OF ORALITY

In addition to storying, or storytelling, there are many different facets of orality and oral art forms. These include chants, drama, song and dance, and the use of poetry, parables, and proverbs. Throughout Church history, many other oral learner-friendly methods have been used (e.g., creeds, confessions, and catechisms). There have also been visual arts such as architecture, icons, and stained-glass windows in the Middle Ages cathedrals. These weren't just for decoration but also for communication and instruction. In addition to those methods, we now have radio, television, cell phones, the Internet, recording devices, and many other technological resources today.

As valuable as the technological resources are, some mission groups emphasize making sure that the training methods and strategies are not dependent upon technology. Living Water International basic orality training workshop: An Introduction to Contextual Bible Storying is designed to get people to follow Jesus. It is sometimes referred to as a low-barrier entry, a jumpstart, or an easy-on ramp to the orality movement. After people are on the journey, many other resources are introduced, primarily through the International Orality Network, the Evangelical Missiological Society, Missio Nexus, and many others.

Other important aspects of Orality practices and training methods are the need to understand the receptor culture, worldview, and contextualization. It's also helpful to give attention to language, learning preferences, behavior change, and related disciplines such as sociology, psychology, anthropology, theology, epistemology, and other aspects of missiology. It's helpful to know the depth and breadth of the movement and the multiple disciplines involved.

One of the concerns that many express is, "How can the accuracy of the message be maintained without having written forms?" That is a great question, and with a little study of oral cultures and traditions, we can appreciate how God not only inspired His written Word but how He has preserved and maintained its accuracy in oral form before it became a written text. Most scholars agree that much of the Bible was communicated orally for a considerable length of time before it was written down.

Thankfully, in many places where orality training and strategies are taking place today, there are some who are literate and have access to the Scriptures. However, in primarily oral cultures where there is no Scripture in their language, more repetition and a focus on learning in the community can maximize maintaining the accuracy of the biblical message. Something we often see in our orality training programs in Africa, Asia, and Latin America, and to some extent in the West, is the benefit of shared knowledge and the collective memory of the group or community. Seeing how people come alive with new passion and confidence for sharing the Good News of Jesus and making disciples during training in teams and communities is exciting.

TEAM-BASED DISCIPLE-MAKING

One of the things we've seen work well is training teams to train as teams. We emphasize that no one person must remember everything, but each person can tell as much as they can remember with the help of the group. The participants see this demonstrated in the basic orality training, where they hear a story told several times, with some explanation of the background and context. Then, they discuss what they see as the main message, the important lessons, and how they apply to their lives. Our focus is on obedience-based disciple-making. It's not just about knowledge and information, but life change. It's about hiding the Word in our hearts so that it becomes part of our lives.

People are often amazed and surprised to discover how much they can learn from a few short stories, with the appropriate pre- and post-story discussion and dialogue. In fact, we tell people that with five stories from the Gospels, we can give a community, village, or tribal group a simple, systematic narrative theology of the most important things they need to know to have a relationship with the living God and become reproducing followers of Jesus.

Another important aspect is to determine how much and what they need to know and what is the best delivery system? That not from two centuries of Church history, but from the Scriptures, especially from the life, teaching, and Spirit of Jesus. In places where there are more educated and biblically knowledgeable pastors and Church leaders, we can go deeper with discussions around topics like:

- *What is a disciple?*
- *When does a person become a disciple?*
- *What do disciples do?*
- *What is a Church or community of faith?*
- *What do Churches exist for?*

While orality methods and strategies are vital in international and cross-cultural missions, especially among unreached and unengaged people groups, we see a growing interest in the Global North and Western World. Pastors and Church leaders initially became interested in orality training and the use of storytelling for their short-term mission trips. However, once they see how it works, they recognize that it is universal in its application and will work right in their Churches and communities. As we have noted before, there are many oral preference learners in North America and the West.

In many parts of the world, women and children have little opportunity to participate in the life of the Church. Orality training allows everyone to participate and engage. When pastors observe young children and women who have had little or no formal education learn and retell stories, they begin to catch a vision of how they can equip, train, and mobilize storytelling evangelists and disciple makers at every level of education and socio-economic status.

Increasingly, as Churches and ministries in North America have become aware of and interested in orality methods and strategies, pastors and leaders are seeing the benefit in their congregations and organizations. In addition to training those on short-term mission trips, they realize the impact it can have with outreach, small groups, children, prison ministries, nursing homes, street gangs, and much more. Using story-based sermons is catching on with some pastors and Church leaders, who are reporting very encouraging results.

Someone has said that the Gospel started in the early Church like a ping pong ball, and now it's like a bowling ball. In order for it to be understandable, reproducible, and transferable to any place and all people groups, we need to peel back some of the nonessentials. The Good News of Jesus spread throughout the entire populated world, primarily through Orality-based methods, before the printing press, radio, TV, and many of the resources we enjoy today.

A GREAT NEW VISTA IN THE WORLD MISSION

In his foreword to *Beyond Literate Western Models*, Douglas Birdsall, honorary chairman of the Lausanne Committee on World Evangelization, refers to Orality as a great new vista in world missions. He wrote, "It also opens the doorway to train and deploy great numbers of people who will be able to tell the Greatest Story in fresh and creative ways to those who have never heard. This is about as exciting and compelling as it gets in the great enterprise of world missions."

When we take our Lord's Great Commission seriously, we need to take into consideration the role of orality in disciple-making, Church growth, and communicating the good news of Jesus. It is normal to think in terms of our own cultural context, but our thinking needs to be focused on those who need it the most, the least, and the last of the unreached people. Jesus didn't say to make disciples of all literate people groups, but all people. In recent years orality has become an important topic among Bible translation organizations, and literacy training programs. The concepts and principles of orality are the vanguard of all other strategies. Orality methods are the most ancient and universal ways that people have communicated, learned, and processed information from the beginning of time.

CONCLUSION

The most common Orality-based method for learning and communicating is storytelling. Narrative theology and narrative preaching are becoming important topics among pastors, teachers, ministry, and Church leaders. Properly understood in the biblical context is a powerful concept. Bible storying or storytelling is universal, and it works everywhere. There are stories and traditions among oral cultures that have been passed down from generation to generation. In many places, we are simply giving them better stories that can change lives and transform communities.

In our modern world, there are many different ways that stories can be told or communicated. Typically, our Lord's Great Commission is understood to be going into the world, preaching the Gospel to every person and making disciples of all nations or people groups. Scholars tell us that the word 'preach' in the English Bible comes from about ten different words in the original language. They can all be summed up into one word. That word is to communicate and could include parables, proverbs, poetry, stories, and other oral art forms. In old English, the word Gospel was translated to "good story" or "good news." The more common usage has become good news. So, we could actually sum up the Great Commission in this way, go into all the world and communicate the good story to everyone, and make disciples among all people.

Chapter 16

How is Disciple-Making different from Discipleship?

A SIMPLE STORY

Jesus had been teaching a large crowd of people all day on the shore of the Sea of Galilee. At the end of the day, when evening came, Jesus said to his disciples, "Let us go over to the other side of the lake."

So, leaving the crowd behind, the disciples took him along in the boat just as he was. There were also other boats with them. A furious storm came up over the sea, and the wind and the waves were so strong that it was about to turn the boat over.

Jesus was sleeping in the back of the boat on a cushion. The disciples woke Jesus up and said, "Rabbi, teacher don't you care that we are about to die?"

Jesus got up, rebuked the wind, and spoke to the waves; he said, "Quiet! Be still!" Then the wind died down, and it was completely calm.

He said to his disciples, "Why are you so afraid? Where is your faith?" The disciples were amazed and terrified and asked each other, "Who is this? Even the wind and the waves obey him!"

This story is recorded in the Gospel of Mark. It can also be found in Matthew and Luke. It is one of the Bible storying and orality training stories and can bring out many lessons and spiritual truths. As we process this story, we ask questions like, "What can we learn from the statement Jesus made, 'Let us go over to the other side of the lake.' After some discussion, we usually conclude that a lesson is that Jesus gives direction and instruction to His followers. Then the disciples took him just as he was in the boat and preceded to go to the other side.

So, they responded to the words of Jesus, which shows us a lesson about instant obedience. They didn't have a discussion, a committee meeting or a focus group but immediately obeyed Him. After retelling the story several times, we discuss things like what we observe, what we can learn, and how it applies to our lives. This is about obedience-based disciple-making, not just learning facts.

Another question we use is, "What do we learn from the fact that Jesus was sleeping during this storm." We point out that if most of us were teaching a large crowd all day, we would be tired and sleepy. So, we learn something about the humanity of Jesus. This story can be used to point out the uniqueness of Jesus. He was never ever less than God but lived like he was never more than man. He was man, as He, as God, created and intended man to be. He was and is the God-man. The fact that He took authority over nature tells us about his deity. Many deep spiritual truths can be discovered in this, and other short stories from Scripture.

What can we learn from the fact that the disciple went to Jesus and said, "Don't you care that we are about to drown or die." In an Orality Training in Rwanda, while discussing this question, a Bible College trained American said, "Those disciples had not been discipled." That comment generated a very healthy discussion about disciples, discipleship, and disciple-making. Discussing these kinds of questions can bring out many insights and helpful lessons. They can also help clarify many misconceptions people might have. It has been our experience that many people today have faulty ideas about these matters based on various religious traditions rather than the Scriptures. This interactive and participatory learning helps people get back to a biblically based understanding.

LIVING OUT AND SHARING HIS LIFE

Think about what we can learn from this short story that helps us distinguish between disciple-making and the modern term of discipleship. Many people today, especially in the North American context, think of discipleship as a program, a class, or a curriculum. The term discipleship is less than 200 years old. Discipleship was a term coined by Charles Adams in the 1850s, which resulted in a dichotomy between evangelism and discipleship. There is no such distinction in Scripture. Making disciples is more about an impartation of life. Of course, that is the life of God that brings people into a living relationship with the Lord. There is a big need in the Church today to have a more biblical understanding of how Jesus made disciples and what He has called us to do. Making disciples begins by living out and sharing Christ's life with others. Introducing people to Jesus and getting them on the journey of following Him is not as complicated as some have come to believe.

In reality, when we have introduced someone to Jesus and they come into a personal relationship with the living Christ, we have made a disciple. The question then becomes, what is next and what else can we do to nurture them in that relationship. A lady in the Central African

Republic participated in an orality training. The evening after the first day of training, she told this story of Jesus calming the storm to some ladies in the marketplace. After hearing and discussing the story, one of the ladies in the group said, "I see that in this storm (difficult time), those disciples went to Jesus." She said, "For me, I see that I should be going to Jesus instead of the witch doctor. So, from now on, I'll be going to Jesus when I face difficult times."

That is a good example of how the Holy Spirit gives people insight, understanding, and applications of the Scripture. We often say you don't have to be a great storyteller because we have great stories to tell. When we tell these stories, accurate from the Scriptures, the Holy Spirit will touch people's hearts and change their lives.

A retired schoolteacher, who attended a few orality training workshops, became interested in becoming a trainer improving her skills at disciple making. So, she participated in Living Water International's Orality Training for Trainers. She shares how the Lord often uses this story of Jesus calming the storm in her life. When she is in a traffic jam, dealing with a problem, or some troubling situation, the Lord brings to her mind these questions that Jesus asked his disciples. "Why are you so afraid? Where is your faith?" She says that brings her comfort and peace in those times. In our training sessions, we use this part of the story to talk about the connection between fear and faith and how perfect love casts out fear.

Another discussion question that can be asked in the training or in casual conversation with someone is, what can we learn from the question the disciples asked Jesus, "Don't you care that we are about drown? Many people today ask similar questions, does God care about me and my situation. Of course, the answer is yes. Not only does He care, but He can also change our lives, circumstances, and destinies.

When we know He cares, we are more likely to call on him in times of need.

CHANGING THE FACE OF MISSIONS

Many Church and Mission leaders today say that the orality movement is transformational in Church history and one of the most significant developments in Kingdom advancement in the past 500 years. Orality is also the fastest-growing movement in evangelism today, and it is changing the face of missions around the world.

Orality methods and strategies are amazingly effective ways of communicating the Gospel and making disciples. However, they also enhance efforts in relationship building, community development, business as mission, leadership training, integral mission, and more. Simplicity and reproducibility are key factors that make these methods universal and transferable to any culture around the world. Appropriate orality and storying training can equip believers to go anywhere, with just what is in their heads and hearts, and reproduce it in the heads and hearts of others. It can cross all barriers and borders.

According to the Lausanne Movement and the International Orality Network, more than 80 percent of the world's population are considered oral learners by necessity or preference. Oral learners communicate through storytelling, drama, songs, poetry, parables, proverbs, and other oral art forms. Ironically, 90 percent of the world's Christian workers present the Gospel using literate—not oral—communication styles. In order to reach and disciple oral learners, we must learn to use strategies that are familiar and relevant to them.

A SCHOLAR'S PERSPECTIVE

Dr. Tom Steffen, professor emeritus of intercultural studies at Biola University, director of the Doctor of Missiology program, former missionary, and author of several books on missions and cross-cultural ministry, writes about the Orality Movement going global. He says, "The modern Orality movement impacts global ministry on every level, whether one is aware of it or not. It influences every aspect of ministry: training, theological education, Bible curricula, Bible translation, evangelism, Church planting, community development, business as mission, creation care, the arts, media, hermeneutics, and homiletics. Let us hope that global Church leaders discover its contributions. The present Orality movement can provide many answers for global ministries if we can shed our silos."

Several years ago, I had the privilege of being part of a round table discussion with some key Christian leaders. The gathering was in preparation for a Fasting and Prayer event in Houston led by Dr. Bill Bright, founder of Campus Crusade for Christ. In addition to Dr. Bright, others in the meeting were Dr. Doug Hodo, then president of Houston Baptist University (now Houston Christian University), and a few other city leaders and mega Church pastors. I have vivid memories of that meeting. One was a topic of discussion Bill Bright initiated. In conversation, he went around the room and asked each man this question. "How did you come to Christ? And, who discipled you?"

The most interesting thing was hearing each man's answer to those questions. Each one had a unique story about how they came to the Lord. None of them pointed to any one person or plan in the ways they were discipled. Hearing these man, each were prominent leaders in the Church world, share their experiences led me to think of how creative and unlimited the Holy Spirit is in working in our lives and maturing us in our relationships with Him. The Lord Jesus is the ultimate disciple maker, and He lives in each of us to carry out His purposes.

GREAT RESOURCES FOR DISCIPLE-MAKING

There are an amazing number of resources available to believers these days to help in our spiritual journeys. I have been blessed to use several of them. It is ideal for every new convert to have a more mature believer to mentor and guide them. However, many still need that option. The encouraging thing is knowing that Christ Himself, through the Holy Spirit, can disciple, nurture and instruct us on our spiritual journey. Many times, He uses someone else in that process. We can have confidence that the Spirit will guide us into all truth. Philippians 1:6 tells us, "Being confident of this, that He who began a good work in us will carry it on to completion until the day of Christ Jesus."

Many people think of discipleship as a program, a curriculum, a set of principles, or a class. However, biblical disciple-making is more about the impartation of life and relationships. First, of course, is a relationship, a spiritual union, with God. Then our relationships with other members of the Body of Christ. Jesus spent time with His followers, conversing and giving instructions, usually in small groups. While He occasionally spoke to the masses, most of His time was in person with the few.

Many books, instructional materials, audio and video programs, and digital media resources are available in our modern Western English-speaking world. They are all helpful and effective in their appropriate context. I like to promote the idea of using all means available. Yet, many have had the best resources and great personal mentoring and still depart from the faith. However, with little outside help and a minimum of resources, others grow in their relationship with Christ and produce much fruit. It is a testimony to the faithfulness of God to all who submit to the Lordship of Christ and obey whatever light they may have. When one responds to and obeys the light they have, God will see to it that they receive more. Also, as we give others what the Lord has given us, He will multiply back. That applies to material possessions as well as spiritual truth.

CONCLUSION

So many people think of discipleship as a complicated process that requires a theological education or a certain level of biblical knowledge. When, in fact, it is not as difficult as we might think. It is often valuable to consider what a disciple is and how someone becomes a disciple. Actually, a disciple is a learner or follower. To overcome the common stigma of discipleship, as opposed to disciple-making, it is helpful to reevaluate these concepts based on the clear teachings of Scripture. Some modern Western Church traditions have often created some confusion regarding these topics.

I'd like to reiterate, because this is an important point that, when we have introduced someone to a vital relationship with the living Christ, in reality, we have made a disciple. An important question is, what do we do next? How can we encourage them on the journey to spiritual maturity? As followers of Jesus, we should be on a life-long journey of growing in grace and knowledge of God. The truth is, once a person has had a life-changing encounter with Christ and understands the Gospel, they can introduce others to Him and get them on the journey. The reproducing life of the risen Lord Jesus in and through each of His children is what matters most.

Chapter 17

Why the Concepts and Principles of Orality are Crucial for Completing the Great Commission

It was in the early 1980's that I came across Herbert Klem's book *Oral Communication of the Scripture: Insights from African Oral Art*. I was working with an international publishing and broadcasting organization at the time. It was a time of recognizing that what I was doing was effective with only about twenty-thirty percent of the world's population. I then connected with a few mission leaders with some experience with or interest in orality, oral cultures, and reaching oral learners and unreached people groups. Those years put me on a new path of discovery and understanding about what it will take to reach the whole world and complete the Great Commission.

In collaboration with others during the 1980's and 1990's about the use of oral methods for sharing the Gospel and making disciples, I found a few who were interested and some with practical experience. At an Evangelism Roundtable Conference in Washington, D.C., a Church growth leader took an interest in what I was doing and invited me to present a workshop on "Oral Discipleship" at a major conference in the summer of 1988 called 'Chicago '88.' The conference was attended by several thousand pastors, evangelists, missionaries, and Church/mission leaders. This was a season of significant changes in the global church and especially in mission strategies.

The workshop I led at the Chicago '88 event was based on my personal experimentation, research, and a concept paper I had written in 1983, titled *Oral Discipleship: A Strategy of Evangelism and Discipleship Designed to Reach Primarily the Non-Reading People of the World, Using Oral (Verbal) Methods* (The term Orality was not commonly being used at that time). A few years ago, I discovered that my workshop at that conference had been archived at the Billy Graham Center at Wheaton College. Samuel Chiang, former executive director of the International Orality Network, credits me with coining the term "Oral Discipleship" (although I now prefer the term Disciple-Making, rather than Discipleship as explained in an earlier chapter).

I have been on an ongoing learning journey for those years and have connected with many others. My research and experimentation during the 1980's and 1990's provided a good foundation for my work in launching our contextual Bible storying and orality training programs with Living Water International. We began with Bible storying training and practices in 2006, then followed up by launching our first orality training workshops in 2009 in Liberia and Honduras. The first rendition we called 'An Introduction to Contextual Bible Storying.' Following those early days of experimentation and refining, we took the training to all our program countries throughout Africa, Central and South America, and Asia.

It's been remarkable to receive feedback and reports of how the training has spread to many other countries by those who have received the training. In subsequent years, we have also conducted the training in many churches throughout the United States. Many of those churches have had much success with using the stories on their mission trips to Latin America, Africa and Asia. One church has trained pastors in Southeast Asia, India and Ethiopia. When pastors are trained, it spreads rapidly, especially among house church movements in some of the creative access countries.

BIBLE STORYING: AN EASY ON-RAMP TO THE ORALITY MOVEMENT

Contextual Bible storying has come from considerable research and gleaning from many other Bible storying and orality-based methods and models. Chronological Bible storying was the most commonly used method at that time. However, we also gleaned concepts and principles from relational Bible storying, thematic Bible storying, topical Bible storying, panoramic Bible storying, and conversational Bible storying to name a few. Another important feature of this model is emphasizing the appropriate biblical and cultural contexts.

Over time, we began to experience a growing interest in Orality from Living Water International's short-term mission trips and supporting Churches. In 2010 we began conducting Bible storying and orality training workshops for Churches, mission organizations, and with academic institutions throughout the United States. Initially, pastors and mission leaders became interested in training for those going on short-term mission trips. Then, as they saw its effectiveness and impact, they began to discover applications in their local Churches and communities. In the process of time, a good number of US-based Churches began conducting their own orality training events. Some are finding the training effective with various outreaches, including assisted living facilities, prison ministries, refugee and immigrant communities, as well as international students, to name a few.

A transformational lesson is learning more about the power of collective memory in training and practice. The more relational, communal, oral cultures in the Global South are providing many lessons for those of us in the Global North. We recognize the rapidly reproducing disciple-making and Church planting movements are primarily in those regions. Small, simple, and reproducible systems and structures are concepts we need more of here in the United States. In many ways, the orality movement is creating greater awareness that there may be better ways of advancing the Gospel than the common practices over the past 500 years. Back to basics is a common theme we are hearing these days, and rediscovering that the ancient ways of biblical times and the early church are effective in our modern times.

Living Water International's basic orality training (An Introduction to Contextual Bible Storying) uses a five-story set. It was not designed to be a comprehensive training, but to be a sample, to get people on the journey. It is an easy on-ramp, or low barrier entry, to the Orality Movement. In our experience, with the five stories from the Gospels, with the appropriate pre- and post-story discussion and dialogue, we can give a village, a community, or a tribal group a simple, biblical theology of what it means to have a relationship with the Lord and become reproducing followers of Jesus. Part of that process is to move away from an exclusively Modern Western, Post-Reformation perspective to a more biblical, Early Church and Global South mental model.

SIGNIFICANT INFLUENCES IN THE MOVEMENT

Some of the helpful resources and influences in the formative stages of our orality training programs and strategies would include the works of many including:

- Trevor McIlwain
- Mark Naylor

- James Slack
- Mark Snowden
- Tom Steffen
- J.O. Terry
- Avery Willis
- Thomas Winger

As was mentioned earlier, Herbert Klem's doctoral dissertation on *Oral Communication of the Scriptures* was a catalyst and inspiration to many of us on the Orality journey. Amsterdam 2000, Table 71, and the formation of the Oral Bible Task Force (forerunner of the International Orality Network) have all been significant influences that have accelerated the Orality Movement.

After hearing the story of the Gerasene man with the evil spirits from Mark 5, a woman in the training in Nicaragua approached one of the pastors and said, "I'm like that man; I need help." It turned out that she had been involved with witchcraft. After a time of prayer and deliverance that evening, the next day, she was calm and learning with the group. There are so many compelling stories and testimonies like these that could fill several books. It is an incredible faith building experience when we see the truth of the accounts in the Bible lived out and experienced in people's lives.

After observing the impact of the basic orality training within Living Water International's program areas, we moved to a new level of training trainers. The orality training for trainers took us to a new, more accelerated, multiplying impact level. This concept of training is based on training teams to train as teams. Through collaboration with the International Orality Network, and other mission networks and associations, we now have access to a wealth of knowledge and experience about orality's many aspects and applications. Our global community of learning and practice continues to grow from our collective experience and lessons learned with Living Water International, and their many affiliates and partners.

One of the big challenges is tracking and reporting, the results of orality training and practices. However, with the story-impact tool and the most significant change model, we have a much better way of tracking, reporting and measuring impact. The monitoring and evaluation programs have provided much better ways of documenting and demonstrating impact. Other groups have been good resources for determining the metrics to measure impact and spiritual metrics. There is no shortage of anecdotal examples and stories. Since most of our training experiences are in oral cultures, many need more capacity or resources to report results. However, when we return to those areas and interview some trainees, the stories and numbers are quite impressive.

RAPIDLY SPREADING THE GOSPEL

A senior leader with the Evangelical Fellowship of Zimbabwe participated in Living Water's orality training for trainers 2013. During an International Orality Network Africa Regional Consultation in South Africa in 2018, he reported that since that time, he had trained more than 4,000 pastors with that basic model. Furthermore, according to the reporting of EFZ, those 4,000 pastors had trained more than 400,000 others. In Burkina Faso, we have received reports of how the training has greatly accelerated their Church planting efforts. The Churches meet under trees, and pastors have had little or no theological training. They are an example of how orality strategies can be used for rapidly spreading the Gospel and enhancing disciple-making movements.

Over the past few years, orality methods and strategies have been expanded into several other areas of application. Communicating the Gospel and making disciples are the most basic applications. However, principles of orality are amazingly effective in hygiene education, public health, and community development. In 2017 a program for Contextualized Leadership Development for Oral Cultures was launched in Kenya. It has since been simplified to what is now called Orality Leadership Workshops. The idea is to equip pastors and other leaders with the best leadership skills from contemporary, historical, and biblical resources. Again, our best model for effective leadership is the life, Spirit, and teaching of Jesus. While knowledge and skill are important, the primary focus is character development. Guided discovery, action learning, and participatory models of learning are also extremely valuable in this arena.

The collaboration and shared learning among various mission and ministry organizations continue to enhance our global community of learning and practice. We are also experiencing many opportunities of bringing these methods and strategies into other networks, alliances, and associations. A few of those include the Global Alliance for Church Multiplication, the Christian Leadership Alliance, the Global CHE Network (sponsor of the annual International Wholistic Mission Conference), Missio Nexus, Mission ConneXion conferences, the Accord Network, the Millennial Water Alliance, Church Planting Networks, and others. The International Orality Network's affiliation with the Lausanne Movement and the World Evangelical Alliance had provided fruitful collaboration and shared learning opportunities.

STRATEGIC RESOURCE LEVERAGING

All these developments are leading to greater opportunities for strategic leveraging of impact for Kingdom advancements. According to Dr. Steve Douglas, former President of Cru, Orality is a game changer for global mission strategies for unreached people groups, but also for local ministries and reaching the nations among us. As the movement gains visibility, and credibility, there is increased interest among educators and academic communities. In fact, we are continually identifying valuable scholarly work that has been around for many years but not very visible and has not been implemented into contemporary mission/ministry strategies.

Still in its early stages, the Orality Missiology Collaboration Group consists of a growing number of practitioners, trainers, researchers, and scholars. Now, it also includes several doctoral candidates doing dissertations on orality and related topics. In our research efforts, we are discovering seminaries, universities, and other institutions of higher education with excellent programs that fit within the orality domain. Some of those include areas such as ethnomusicology, ethno-doxology, ethno-dramatology, and theological aesthetics. Other disciplines or fields of study related to orality include narratology, oral traditions, Early Church history, linguistics, cross-cultural studies, oral literature, and worldview issues. There is growing recognition within the orality mission community and educational institutions that many resources are available to enable one to understand of this important field of learning and practice. Another recent development is the creating of an orality studies program with the Asia Graduate School of Theology based in Manila, Philippines.

Progressively, we are experiencing a growing interest and recognition of the multiple applications of the principles of orality. An example would be our networking and collaboration with the Business as Mission Movements. Orality is being effectively used in team building and improving corporate culture. Howard Partridge has participated in Living Water's orality training and applied it to his coaching and consulting businesses. He is well known for his expertise through his work with Phenomenal Products and the Zig Zigler organization. Among several books he has authored, he addresses the use of his Orality Training in *The Power of Community*. Concepts of Orality can enhance corporate culture, sales, marketing, organizational change, leadership, and management.

NETWORKING AND CROSS-POLLINATION

Through networking and cross-pollination, we continue to discover additional applications. Some of those would include trauma therapy, racial reconciliation, conflict resolution, and promoting unity and cooperation, to name a few. A businessman with a long history of mission work, locally and globally, participated in multiple orality training events. He has been involved with stewardship, financial management, and planning training. After receiving the basic orality training and orality training for trainers, he adapted his model to a more oral learner-friendly approach. He first tested it in Africa, where they saw a more rapid reproduction of the training in several other countries. Then, he also began implementing that simplified model in the United States with improved results. Some key changes and lessons learned were, reducing the content, more repetition, more engagement, focus on communal participatory learning, and less dependency on written materials.

International Orality Network conferences and consultations over the past few years have also brought attention to various other disciplines and applications. Honor and Shame was the focus of a Consultation on Orality in Theological Education hosted by Houston Christian University in 2014. Daystar University in Nairobi, Kenya, hosted a similar consultation in 2015 focusing on practitioners and trainers. Several other such consultations have occurred in Hong Kong, Wheaton, Asbury, Oklahoma, Oxford, England, Manila, Philippines, Togo, West Africa, Johannesburg, South Africa, and others. In the North America Regional context, annual conferences have been in Houston, Colorado Springs, Orlando, Toronto, Dallas, Saint Louis, and a few other cities. Each gathering enriches participants with greater awareness, networking, learning, collaboration, and partnership opportunities.

Over the past decade, Orality strategies have increasingly become a significant part of Living Water International and its many affiliates and partner programs around the world. In the water sector, WASH has become an important focus. (WASH is an acronym for Water Access, Sanitation, and Hygiene). WASH program areas are also focused on community development and spiritual transformation. In partnership with the Church, locally and globally, Living Water's strategies are known as *Flourish: Mobilizing Churches and Communities for WASH-Focused Transformation*. That program, which also includes Bible Storying and other Orality Training, is not only about sharing the Gospel, disciple-making, and Church planting but has been instrumental in influencing national policy on child marriage in Southern Africa. Orality principles were very effectively used by Living Water workers in Liberia and other West African countries addressing the Ebola crisis a few years ago.

The theme of the Orlando conference in 2018 was 'Orality: Many Applications–One Mandate.' The one mandate, of course, is the Great

Commission. While there are many different aspects to the orality domain and a wide variety of special interests, we like to focus on communicating the Gospel and making disciples as foundational to everything else. In relation to the arts, Artists in Christian Testimony (ACT International) is a key network that specializes in that area. The 2019 Toronto conference emphasized indigenous arts, women's issues, reaching first nations and young leaders. Toronto, the most ethnically diverse city in the world, was an excellent place for those discussions. Houston, now the most ethnically diverse city in the United States.

Several relief and development organizations have been interested in Orality methods and strategies. Some missionaries and mission executives request assistance implementing oral strategies and methods for agriculture, cooking, and nutrition programs. Engineering ministries recognize that Orality-based strategies are effective in their disciple-making efforts and in training practical skills in a cross-cultural context. Program producers and others are realizing the benefits of Orality methods and strategies through connections and relationships with National Religious Broadcasters program. A few recent articles, seminars, and webinars have addressed areas such as Arts and Orality for Wholistic Missions, Orality in Business, The Place of Orality in Church Planting, Oral Strategies for Rapid Multiplication, The Importance of Orality in the Church, Missions and the Academy, Orality in Education, Orality and Missions, Short-term Missions, and Orality in the Academy and Beyond.

Several encouraging developments have occurred over the past few years. Youth and young leaders' increased interest in Orality is growing and spreading. One example is the ION Youth initiative which emerged from the ION Africa Consultation in Johannesburg in 2018. From that gathering, young people in Zambia began conducting their own Orality-focused outreaches and training events. That has also spread to other countries throughout the region.

TOOLS OF THE AGE – TOOLS OF THE AGES

Digital storytelling, online collaboration, and training provide new opportunities for engaging younger leaders. Zoom calls, webinars, and other online orality training workshops are taking on new expressions. Our new foci in the North America Regional context are arts, media, and young leaders. A common theme is using the most effective tools of the age and the tools of the ages. Using all the modern technological resources and the ancient methods we learn from Jesus, the Early Church, and the rapidly reproducing disciple-making and Church planting movements, primarily in the Global South.

Another strategic and impact opportunity in the orality movement is connecting with and supporting children's ministries. Child Evangelism Fellowship, AWANA, and others are beginning to implement story and Orality-based methods. The four to fourteen Window Movement, and its many member organizations, is another example of the expanding and multiplying impact of the orality movement.

We have observed that when children tend to tell stories when they learn stories. Training events often have children as young as five or six years old participate. They often learn and retell the stories, sometimes to groups of several hundred participants. Adults are encouraged and inspired when they see how children can learn the stories so well. A pastor in one of the trainings commented, "I see now how I can equip, train and mobilize storytelling evangelists at every level of education and economic status."

Connecting with prayer networks and prayer movements are also channels for introducing and injecting Orality concepts and principles for accelerating impact. Children's prayer movements in South Asia are growing and have tremendous potential for long-term impact on the Kingdom. Integrating orality methods into women's prayer movements, especially in creative access countries in the Middle East and North Africa, is an area for expanding impact.

CONCLUSION

Why so much emphasis on orality? The more awareness we have of the multi-faceted aspects and multiple applications of these ancient methods that are relevant today, the greater the interest will be to learn more. Pastors, mission leaders and anyone interested in being more effective in witnessing, ministry and disciple making will want to keep an eye on this phenomenon. With more of these resources becoming available, online and well as in person, every believer can access them and make a more significant contribution to completing the great commission.

Chapter 18

Why it is so Consequential to be Flexible, Adaptable, and Open to Change

WE'VE NEVER DONE IT THAT WAY BEFORE

This is a saying we heard a lot a few years ago. It had to do with the last words of a dying Church. It could also apply to an institution, an organization, or a company. It is important these days to be flexible, adaptable, and open to change. During rapidly changing times, we can learn more about walking by faith, not by sight. It's often in seasons of twists and turns of life that we experience God's grace in new and different ways.

A certain segment of the world's population resists change more than others. It may be due to a fear of the unknown or a lack of interest in trying something new or different. Some people like to do things they have always done in the same ways they have always done them. It is human nature to want to do what we are comfortable with. However, if we are going to grow and improve, we need to change and step out of our comfort zones. At times we all must do things that we are not comfortable with. Over the years in ministry, I've noticed that a lot of people like to hear messages that they already know and fully agree with, and that require no lifestyle change. Old habits and traditions often take priority over truth.

In our work with Living Water International around the world, we find that behavior change is one of our biggest challenges everywhere. In some places, people need to be convinced that using and drinking water from a new water well in their community or village is better than going to the river they have been using for years. The comfort zone issue is a worldwide problem. Most people have comfort zones and resist change to some degree.

EXPERIENCING ORALITY

One of the challenges those in the orality movement face is the initial questioning, skepticism, and resistance among some. A few pastors, Church leaders, and more educated people sometimes think orality methods are a step backward because literacy-based academic training has been emphasized in the modern Western models of theological education. Some still think orality and storytelling are bedtime stories for children or the people of the world who are often referred to as illiterate, non-literate, or functionally illiterate. However, rather than defining people based on what they cannot do, many realize we can define them based on what they can do; they are oral learners by necessity or preference. When people are exposed firsthand and experience the depth, breadth, and multi-faceted aspects of the orality movement, they begin to understand and embrace it.

A successful businessman, who participated in an Orality Training Workshop, said, "Of all the conferences, seminars, and training events I have attended over the years, I have never experienced one that is so practical and immediately useful as this one." People are often amazed and surprised at how much we can learn in one day, using no literate-based or technological resources. Living Water International's model is designed and intended to prepare people to go to any place and any people group on the planet, with just what is in their heads and hearts that can be reproduced in the heads and hearts of others.

When pastors and mission leaders take the time to discover the significance of orality, it makes a world of difference. When they personally participate in training, it is often a transformational experience. We have often observed that orality is better experienced than explained, which is why we focus on demonstration, participation, and explanation. There is an age-old problem of not knowing what we don't know. It is an eye-opener when we are exposed to new things that cause us to think differently and realize the value of learning and doing new things. In the case of orality, however, it is not as much a new thing as a rediscovery of ancient ways that have been neglected for the past 500 years or so.

A university professor participated in an orality training event because his daughter, who is an elementary school teacher, invited him. The professor was so impressed that he changed his class room model from lectures to short presentations and included small group discussions. He said the university students loved it and actually learned better.

BETTER EXPERIENCED THAN EXPLAINED

With better research, we now know that more than seventy percent of the world's population are oral learners by necessity or preference. These are the 5.7 billion people who can't, don't, or won't read or prefer to learn by means other than print-based media or written instruction.

People from the United States who go on mission trips often tell us that the cross-cultural experience gives them a new perspective on church life and ministry strategies. Pastors who attend the training often change their preaching style to make it more engaging and interactive. People respond more positively to that style and retain more of the message. They tend to discuss and share the message with others during the week.

The more biblically knowledgeable Church and mission leaders, who have an international and cross-cultural orientation, usually can get their minds around the significance of Orality when confronted with the right questions. The following are a few of the questions that are often eye-openers and give perspective to the movement:

How would you share or communicate the Good News of the Kingdom of God in places where you cannot take literate or technological resources?

- How would you make disciples in places where the people have no literate skills or Scripture in their language?
- What are the most important truths people need to know to enter a relationship with the Living God?
- How much, and what, do people need to know to become reproducing disciple makers (followers of Jesus)?
- What are the most appropriate methods (delivery systems) to communicate these truths to others?
- Who is our best model throughout recorded history as a communicator, trainer, and disciple-maker?
- How can we ensure that our message and methods are biblical, understandable, and reproducible in all places and among all people groups?

The prerequisite to answering these questions needs to be based, not on contemporary Church traditions, but on the Scriptures, with a special focus on the teachings of Jesus and the Early Church. When those questions are properly addressed, we understand how we can go to the ends of the earth, to every place and all people groups, and make disciples in ways that can be reproduced within that people group. We often emphasize that Jesus did not say 'go and make disciples of all literate people groups,' but *all* people groups. No one is excluded.

INTERNALIZING THE WORD OF GOD

From this process, many are concluding that the lessons we learn from the rapidly reproducing disciple-making movements in the developing world will also work in our modern western context. Learning preference and behavior change are important considerations if we want people to internalize the Word of God. Relational, communal, narrative, and participatory methods are amazingly effective ways of carrying out the Great Commission. Cultural value systems and worldview issues are also important considerations. Adapting to the receptor culture will make a world of difference and enhance effectiveness.

Sometimes important lessons can be learned or discovered because of being pushed out of our comfort zones. For example, a pastor was in the middle of his sermon at a Church service, and the lights went out. He may not have thought he was prepared to continue, but he did so because he had no choice. He was amazed at how much he could remember without his notes. That was a valuable experience that was beneficial for years to come.

A missionary was in a country where an armed conflict was taking place. He had the opportunity to share the Gospel and do some Bible teaching with a group of local people at night. Because of the possibility of hostile fire from a rebel group active in the region, they could not use lights of any kind. So, they were limited to sharing and teaching only what they could remember. The missionary shared with great excitement how effective his Orality Training had prepared him for that situation.

Another mission worker shared that a rebel group had stolen their Jesus film equipment. He said that they had received Orality Training a few months earlier, so they were equipped to share the Gospel using only Bible stories and oral methods. The rebel group could not steal the message of the Word of God that was hidden in their hearts.

GOD AT WORK IN DIFFICULT TIMES

So often, difficult times or crisis situations provide some of the most fruitful witness and ministry opportunities. However, we can seek to find common ground and bring Jesus into our conversations, even before bad things happen. The Lord is faithful to do so as we pray and trust Him for wisdom and direction. If we consistently sow the Seed of His Word and share our God stories and testimonies, we can have confidence that occasionally we'll connect with fertile soil.

It is encouraging to receive feedback and reports of the work of God in people's lives we've shared with. I recently reconnected with a man I led to the Lord more than thirty years ago. He was a next-door neighbor for only one year. During that time, we had multiple conversations about the Lord and spiritual matters. You could call it a mentoring or discipling relationship. Since those days, this former neighbor has been instrumental in many family members and friends coming to the Lord. In fact, some became actively involved in ministry. It is an example of the reproducing life of the Lord Jesus in and through each of us who follow and trust Him.

When we think of our mandate to communicate the Good News of Jesus and make disciples, it's encouraging to know that the Lord will use each of us in that effort. It's ultimately the reproducing life of the Lord Jesus in and through us that produces lasting fruit. The normal Christian life is the realization that it's "not I, but Christ" that produces much fruit for the Kingdom of God (See Gal. 2:20). When we are abiding in Christ, we can expect much fruit, according to John 15.

I received an email from a man who participated in one of Living Water International's Orality Training Workshops a few years ago. He also participated in advanced Orality Training for Trainers . He reported how those he had trained were now training others. They were experiencing a reproducing and multiplying impact. We often hear how the training is being reproduced to four or five, or more generations. Orality strategies are having a ripple effect around the world. The concepts and methods of Orality are effective with our neighbors, our networks, and the nations because they make the message of the Bible understandable, and reproducible.

Something as ordinary as going for a walk in the neighborhood can connect us with people who need the Lord or could use some encouragement. We often refer to this as Prayer-Walking, which is more than prayer and more than walking. Simple gestures of kindness are often all it takes to open conversations that can lead to opportunities of sharing our life in Christ. On average, one out of four people will usually be open to spiritual conversations. It's simple and something everyone can do.

THE NATIONS AMONG US

Our opportunities to our neighbors that can impact the nations are quite remarkable. In a place like Houston, we have the nations among us. In fact, just in the neighborhood where I live, there are people from countries in Asia, Africa, and Latin America. All of them, of course, have relational networks of family, work associates, and others, locally and back in their home countries. So, reaching and discipling one person can often open a whole new network of witness and ministry possibilities.

Almost every witness or ministry opportunity starts with some human connection. Those connections can take on many forms of expression. Today the availability of modern technology can be used to connect with people and communicate the love and message of Jesus. Phone conversations, conference calls, emails, and text messages all present opportunities for reaching and impacting people.

Over the years, I've been able to share the Good News of Jesus and pray with people in many different situations. However, most witness and ministry opportunities usually happen in those normal traffic patterns and our existing relational networks. A key factor is simply being available, watching for opportunities, and being willing to speak up and take action.

A few years ago, a pastor came across my first book, *How to Win Others to Christ.* He later invited me to lead a training in the Church where he served. That turned out to be a life-changing experience for the pastor and, eventually, for the congregation. The pastor told me later that he previously never thought of sharing the Gospel with people outside of his Church field. After reading the book and receiving the training, he started sharing the Lord wherever he went. Shortly after the training in his church, he made a trip across the country. On that trip he shared the gospel and led two people to the Lord. That got him started on a new journey of regularly witnessing. He began seeing people come to Christ on a regular basis, and his excitement impacted many others in his congregation and beyond.

In the context of witness and ministry, I've often heard the phrase, "It's better caught than taught." Years ago, I got to know a few individuals who were filled with joy and excitement about sharing Christ. It sparked a change in my life and put me on a new path of actively sharing with others. That passion for knowing and sharing Jesus has been reproduced in many others over the past few decades.

It is great to realize that the reproducing life of the Lord Jesus, by the work of the Holy Spirit, produces lasting fruit. We get to be His vessels and instruments for advancing His Kingdom. The truth about us is that God intends us to be the truth about Him to those around us. It is the "Not I, but Christ" reality of Galatians 2:20 that makes all the difference. However, true spiritual growth means change. As has been mentioned earlier, every living thing, if it's healthy, grows, changes and reproduces.

While there are so many needs and problems in the world today, all of them represent opportunities. We simply need spiritual eyes to see and ears to hear what the Lord is doing and saying about the opportunities before us each day. He is the same yesterday, today, and forever, and He is working all things after the counsel of His will. The greater the need, the greater the opportunity. We often need to be able to see past the seen and temporary to the not seen and eternal.

In 1990 a group of people went on a mission trip to East Africa and became aware of the great need for clean water. Mission trips to the underdeveloped parts of the world are often great places to learn how to be flexible, adaptable and open to change. That mission trip sparked an interest among the trip participants to do something about it and resulted in the founding of Living Water International. Since its founding, more than 23,000 water projects have been completed to date in Africa, Asia, and Latin America. Millions of lives have been saved and changed through Water and the Word.

History is filled with examples of how problems and needs have created opportunities. The bigger the need, the bigger the opportunity. Think of all the organizations, institutions, and movements that started because someone had a need, a problem or faces some crisis situation. God brings things into our lives, not only for our own growth and benefit but for the benefit of others.

CONCLUSION

Being flexible, adaptable, and open to change is about walking in the Spirit and living by faith. Scripture tells us that we are to walk by faith, not by sight. The just shall live by faith, and without faith, it is impossible to please God. When that is a reality in our lives, we can expect God to work in ways that we have never thought of. A friend likes to say, "God always has something up His sleeve, and He has great big sleeves." It is so easy to get in a rut of doing certain things in a certain way and want to stay in our comfort zone. However, God may desire to break us out of our comfort zones and do new things in and through us. God's mercies are new every morning, and great is His faithfulness. Baptism is a picture of our being buried with Christ in death and raised in the newness of life.

Epilogue

It's a vivid memory of the first time that I knew I was responsible for someone else coming to faith in Christ. During my freshman year in college, I made friends with a Japanese foreign exchange student named Asada. He was a Judo Black Belt who wanted to learn Karate. He learned that I had earned a Black Belt in Karate while serving in the United States Air Force in Japan and Pakistan. The Lord gave me a natural affinity with him. Being fresh out of the Air Force, I had just started a Karate Institute on campus, and Asada joined my first class. We agreed that I would teach him Karate, and he would teach me Judo. He had never learned to drive or had never owned a car. So, I taught him how to drive and helped him buy a car. Over the course of time, he became interested in Christianity and was asking a lot of questions. Not being confident to do so myself, I introduced him to one of my professors, Frank Shell, who led Asada to the Lord. Frank Shell was one of the godliest men I knew at the time, and I was sure he could share the Gospel and introduce Asada to Christ, which he did.

As I later reflected on my experience with Asada, I wondered, "Why didn't I just lead him to Christ myself?" I was probably like many others who feel inadequate or unprepared. When in fact, once we have had a genuine encounter with the living Christ and have responded to the Gospel, we have something to share. A person does not necessarily need to have a lot of biblical knowledge. However, having a basic understanding of the life, death, and resurrection of Jesus, and the need to repent and trust Christ for salvation, they are equipped to be a reproducing follower of Jesus. The Holy Spirit will often use our most feeble efforts in sharing our faith and pointing people to Jesus. It's been a joy over the years to see how a new convert will immediately begin to share their story and the Good News of Jesus. One of the most important things a new follower of Jesus can do is start sharing with others.

In many cases when someone has a genuine new birth experience and received Christ, they will often spontaneously begin sharing their experience with family, friends and others. I witnessed to a lady at a shopping mall one time, and it turned out she was already a believer. She was excited that I approached her to share with her. She immediately told me about her husband who had recently come to the Lord. He was unemployed at the time and had time to share his faith. She said he had led six people to Christ over the past six month. With just a little encouragement, many new converts will take that step of faith and launch out in becoming a reproducing follow of Jesus.

There are many simple stories in Scripture that provide examples and lessons about sharing the Gospel and introducing others to Christ. The account of Jesus' encounter with the Samaritan Woman at the Well, recorded in John 4, is a great example.

After meeting and having a conversation with Jesus the woman left her water pot and went back to her village, telling everyone, "Come, see a man who told me everything I ever did; could this be Christ, the Messiah?" Many believed this because of the testimony of the woman. She basically told a story and asked a question. The people came out to where Jesus was and asked that He stay with them. He stayed for two days, and many more became believers in Jesus. That entire region was eventually impacted by this woman's life and testimony.

We have another lesson in this 4th chapter of John's gospel about sharing our faith. Consider how Jesus initiated His encounter with the woman at the well. He asked a question and found common ground for a conversation. He asked her for a drink of water, then He talked about living water that He gives, that satisfies the deepest thirst. These examples of asking questions and telling stories are effective strategies for us today. Sometimes it can be about telling stories, then asking questions. In this story of the woman at the well, there are many questions that can be asked to bring out many important lessons and applications. Following are a few of those questions:

- How do you think this woman's life was better after encountering Jesus?
- What do you think Jesus meant by Living Water?
- Do you think this woman experienced the Living Water He spoke of?
- What can we learn about sharing our faith from this story?
- Why were the disciples amazed and surprised about Jesus talking to this woman?
- What can we learn about racial or ethnic reconciliation?
- What are some lessons in this story about the character of God?
- Are there lessons in the story about the nature of worship?
- Why did the woman leave her water pot to go back and tell about her encounter with Jesus?
- Have you received and experienced the Living Water Jesus talked about?
- Would you like to receive that Living Water?

There and many spiritual truths and applications in this one story.

JESUS STILL BRINGS CALMNESS IN OUR STORMS OF LIFE

Communicating the Good News of Jesus and making disciples is the essence of our Lord's Great Commission. The account of Jesus Calming the Storm, recorded in Mark 4, is another story that can be used to communicate many spiritual truths and lessons. The fact that Jesus was sleeping in the back of the boat during the storm tells us something about His humanity. Then, later He rebuked the wind and spoke to the wave; He said, "Quiet, be still," and there was complete calm. This speaks of His power of nature and His deity.

These observations can lead to a discussion about the uniqueness of Jesus. He was never ever less than God but lived as though He was never more than man. He was man, as He, as God, intended man to be. When He spoke to the waves provided a lesson about the power of His Word. We often ask, does His Word still have power today? The answer, of course, is yes.

God's Word has power in all forms, spoken, written, or communicated by various oral art forms, such as parables, poetry, proverbs, etc. In our modern world, we have access to many technological and digital resources. An important application is that our words, inspired by the Holy Spirit can have the power to change lives. This gives us greater confidence to reach out and share His Word with others.

In our orality training sessions, we talk about the question the disciples asked Jesus, "Don't you care that we are about to die?" Many people today ask those kinds of questions, does He care about my situation or problems? This story can be used to demonstrate that He does care and He can change our lives and our circumstances. In a Bible Storying training workshop in Zimbabwe, while discussing this story, a lady asked this question; what can we learn from the question the disciples asked each other, "Who is this man, that even the wind and waves obey Him?" She went on to ask, "Didn't they know who he was, they were his disciples?" Many times, the best way to answer a question is with another question. So, I asked the group, what do you think. After some discussion, collectively, the group concluded that the disciples knew who He was but were on a continuing learning journey. The application of the truth is obvious. As followers of Jesus, we are all on a continuing journey of discovering God's wonder, majesty, and greatness in Christ.

The account of Jesus' encounter with the demon-possessed man in the region of the Gerasenes, recorded in Mark 5, is another great example of the impact of a transformed life. A significant truth from this story is how God, not only has power over nature, but also has power over the spirit world.

Demons recognize Jesus as the Son of the Most High God. The fact that He has power over all the gods is especially important in areas with a lot of demonic activity. Jesus commanded the evil spirits to come out of the man, they went into the two thousand pigs and rushed down a steep bluff into the sea, and they all drowned. The herdsmen tending the herd of pigs reported this in the village, and the people came out to see what was happening. When they arrived, they saw the formerly demon-possessed man sitting at the feet of Jesus, fully dressed and in his right mind. (This is a great picture of a transformed life, spiritually, mentally, and physically). The herdsmen were afraid and begged Jesus to leave the region. The formerly demon-possessed man wanted to go with Jesus, but He told him he couldn't. Jesus told him to go back to his people, his hometown, and tell them what great things the Lord had done for him and how He had mercy on him. So, the man went away throughout Decapolis, a region of ten cities, proclaiming and telling the story of what great things the Lord had done for him and how He had mercy on him, and all the people were amazed. This story is another example of how God can use one person to impact a whole region.

Sharing and discussing stories from the Bible is an effective strategy for communicating spiritual lessons and life applications. Sometimes just talking about the stories, even if we don't tell the entire story, can provide opportunities for simple, relational disciple making initiative. Many people who have been exposed to these concepts become very passionate about the possibilities they have for significant kingdom advancing activities. Again, the power of simplicity is somewhat of a lost art in our modern culture.

I like to remind followers of Jesus that the same God who lived in the Lord Jesus more than two thousand years ago now lives in each of us born of the Spirit. Our awareness of that truth and our spiritual union with Christ can give us great confidence that we can be fruitful in every good work and continue to increase in the knowledge of God. There are numerous analogies throughout Scripture that can launch us into greater usefulness to God. It is amazing, once we see these profound truths from Scripture how it can transform our thinking and our lives. The deeper significance of being branches of the True Vine, temples or dwelling places of the Holy Spirit, and ambassadors of Christ, are truths that transform. When we are gripped with the reality of being a new creation, complete and made righteous in Christ, it can compel us to become reproducers of His life. It was coming to an experiential reality of these trues years ago that ignited a new passion in me to share His life with others.

One of my mentors and models in my walk with the Lord was the late Dr. Stephen F. Olford. One of his many books was titled, *"Not I, but*

Christ." That truth from Galatians 2:20, as well as the theme of Christ in You, the hope of glory, from Colossians 1:27, were foundational and the key to experiencing victorious living and fruitful ministry.

For the first five years of my Christian life, I tried to be good and do right. However, with all my efforts, I saw very little fruit. During those early years of trying and working at being what I thought I needed to be, I realized there must be a better way. I came to the point of saying to the Lord, "If you have a better way, I'm ready for it." It was as if the Holy Spirit said, "Thanks, I've been waiting five years for you to discover that, now I can do something with your life."

The late Major W. Ian Thomas was another significant influence in my life that helped me understand this critical truth. He used to say we need to come to the point of admitting to the Lord, "We can't. He never said we could, but He can, and always said He would." Just like we can't save ourselves, we can't live the Christian life apart from Him living it through us. This was revolutionary and transformational for me and has been for many. Sadly, there are so many believers who are living a defeated life, trying, striving, and working hard to be fruitful and victorious in their own strength and resources.

One of the many foundational truths I remember Major Thomas saying was, "The Lord Jesus came into the world to give His life for us, in order to live His life in us, and communicate that life through us." There are many ways of sharing that truth. It is liberating to realize that Jesus Christ is the only one who lived a perfect life. Furthermore, it was the life that He lived that qualified Him for the death that He died, and it was the death that He died that qualifies us for the life that He gives and lives in us.

THE NORMAL CHRISTIAN LIFE

It was a delight to get to know Miss Bertha Smith, a retired missionary who served for many years in China and knew Watchman Nee, author of *The Normal Christian Life*, during the Shantung Revival of 1927-1937. She had many amazing stories from that experience. One of those was how Watchman Nee was influenced by the British Keswick Bible teachers. In fact, many of Nee's sermons and teachings were translated from English into Chinese. Many of his sermons and teachings were later discovered and then translated from Chinese back into English and published in book form. The history of the work of God is inspiring as we realize that He is always a work in any and all situations to advance His Kingdom. God is also prepared to use anyone, regardless of our station in life, to express His character, reveal His will, and communicate His truth. When I think of the normal Christian life, I'm reminded of a quote from Dr. Vance Havner. He said that most Christians are living such sub-normal Christian lives that when someone enters the normal, it may seem like the abnormal. However, God has made adequate provision for every believer to live victorious, fruitful, and reproducing lives.

During the Asbury Revival and Jesus Movement of the early 1970's my wife, Sheila and I got acquainted and made friends with Wayne and Barbara Belt. They were involved with the insurance and real estate business, and both had been deeply impacted by the spiritual movement taking place at the time. Talking about spiritual things and introducing others to Christ seemed to be a very natural and spontaneous part of their lives. Their passion for the Lord was contagious and was a great encouragement to us.

They hosted and led a Bible study in their home every Friday night, made up primarily of college students. It has been remarkable to see how many people came to Christ and were discipled through that gathering, and many ended up going into mission work and ministry. I remember well how Wayne would carry around a briefcase filled with cassette tapes and books that he freely shared with others. He gave me a copy of Jack Taylor's book, *The Key to Triumphant Living*. The Belts are good examples of simple, relational disciple-making and how God uses ordinary followers of Jesus when we have a hunger and thirst for righteousness.

It is a tremendous blessing to have mentors and models in our lives. Personal and up close would be preferable. However, just having access to books and other resources by godly men and women and spiritual leaders can accelerate our growth in the Lord. Finding and following those who have proven track records and fruitful lives and ministries is sometimes more valuable than classroom or academic training.

Also, when it comes to simple, relational disciple-making, methods and techniques are less important than our attitudes and dispositions. When someone has a heart and passion for the Lord, we can trust that He will bring people and resources into our lives to better equip us to honor and please God and walk in His ways. Faithful is He who calls us who will also do it, for it is God who works in us both to will and do of His good pleasure, we are told in Scripture.

APPROACHING AND CLOSING SPIRITUAL CONVERSATIONS

Some may ask the question, what is the most important thing I need to know and do to get on this journey of being a reproducing disciple maker. Of course, it starts with having a settled assurance of our own relationship with the Lord. Then, it's about introducing others to Christ and equipping them to do likewise.

I have learned some important lessons over the past five decades of actively sharing the Gospel, seeking to introduce others to Christ, and get them on the journey of following Jesus. It has been my experience that many believers struggle with two key areas:

1. How to approach people and engage them in spiritual conversations.
2. How to bring people to the point of decision, or to draw the net, so to speak.

There are numerous ways of doing both, and hopefully, the many stories and examples in this book will give anyone some ideas that are useful. In relation to approaching and opening spiritual conversations, there are simple and natural ways to do so. More important than the particular words or methods is a commitment to take action, to act on God's promises. As is mentioned several times throughout this book, God will often give us a unique and creative way we have not known before. When we pray and ask God to prepare our own hearts and give us discernment and sensitivity to the needs of others, we can expect He will answer those prayers Being friendly, treating people with kindness, and asking good questions will go a long way in getting others to engage in meaningful conversations.

I'm often amazed at how the Lord surprises us with those opportunities and divine appointments. The saying that "people don't care how much we know until they know how much we care," is a true statement. Kindness can open many doors in many ways, including opportunities to share the Gospel and make new friends.

Relative to drawing the net, after sharing the Gospel and decerning that a person is responding positively, here are some thoughts that have been helpful for many. When it becomes apparent that someone is ready to embrace the Good News of Jesus, I may say something like the following. The Lord is present with us right now. We don't have to be in a Church building or go through some religious ritual. We can include the Lord in our conversation, and you can call on Him right now. I usually explain from Romans 10 about believing, confessing, and calling on the Lord. He is rich to all who call on Him, and whoever calls on the name of the Lord will be saved. It's also helpful to share from John 3 about what it means to be born again, and John 1 about receiving Christ. Remember also that it's our attitude and trusting the Holy Spirit to direct us and give us the right words that are vital.

In addition to these two aspects about opening and closing those gospel conversations, there is another important part of simple, relational disciple making we should give attention to. That is how to we nurture and encourage those who embrace the gospel to grow and develop in their relationship with the Lord and to become fruitful followers. Also, fruitful followers will eventually become fruitful leaders.

GOD'S TAILOR-MADE METHODS

Just to reiterate and reinforce the importance of these truths. I want to mention that one size doesn't fit all when it comes to sharing the Gospel and making disciples. Being flexible, adaptable, and open to change is important. The Holy Spirit will often give unique and tailor-made strategies for approaching and introducing someone to Christ. Likewise, He will many times give a tailor-made strategy for discipling and getting them on the journey of following Jesus and becoming reproducing disciple-makers. After a person embraces the Gospel and trusts Christ, an important next step is to get them to confess their faith to someone else. Some will be bold and begin to immediately share their faith. Others will need more nurturing, training, and encouragement. There are many books and digital resources available these days to help in these efforts, and they are all effective in their appropriate context. However, having our hearts right with the Lord, trusting Him, and acting in faith is foundational.

Conclusion

One of my long-distance mentors and models was the late Dr. J. Sidlow Baxter. I have fond memories of having lunch with him at a restaurant in Santa Barbara, CA. A ministry colleague and I had a great conversation with him about missions and ministry over lunch. What I remember most about that meeting was our departing company in the parking lot. Dr. Baxter walked us to the car to see us off, and he stood in the parking lot waving goodbye until we were completely out of sight. I can say that Sidlow Baxter was one of the most godly, gracious, and humble men I have ever known. Of the many books he authored, his most popular work was *Explore the Book*, which continues to influence many.

In the providence of God, Leonard Ravenhill was another godly man I had the opportunity to meet and spend time with back in the 1970's. Having the opportunity to be part of a small group for prayer, hearing him preach, and reading his books was a major blessing and encouragement for me. He went to be with the Lord many years ago, but the many books he authored are still having an impact today. Over the course of time, I discovered that Ravenhill sat under the teaching and ministry of Samuel Chadwick. A great quote from Chadwick that I reflect on often is that God often uses the most unlikely candidates to accomplish His most significant work. The complete quotation can be found in his book titled, *The Way of Pentecost*.

Baxter, Ravenhill, and Chadwick departed this earth many years ago and are with the Lord, yet their lives and ministries are still having an impact today. One of the things I have discovered that has been instrumental in discipling others over the years is getting them to read good books that can deepen their faith and increase their fruitfulness. We often hear it said that leadership is basically about influence. That should inspire each of us that we have many different ways of exercising influence in making disciples and advancing the kingdom of God.

SOURCES OF INFLUENCE

Many years ago, the Lord led me to develop a habit that has been one of the most significant practices in my spiritual life and journey. This practice has contributed greatly in relation to learning about being a fruitful witness, communicating the Gospel, making disciples, and equipping and encouraging others to do likewise.

When I get to know or learn about someone who has been greatly used by God, that practice is to find out who were the major influences in their lives. I try to discover what books they have read or what have been the greatest sources and contributions to their spiritual lives. Then I follow up and read some of the same books they have read.

In many cases, one of the best strategies for discipling new converts is introducing them to books and resources to aid in their spiritual growth. James was a man I led to the Lord, and because of location, we were not able to have much contact. So, we corresponded for a period of time, and I recommended books and reading material for him. In addition to his Bible reading, he followed up on my recommendations. He has flourished in his walk with the Lord and had a significant spiritual influence on his family and has been a faithful witness to many others over the past four decades. I suppose we could call that strategy distance discipling. Now days we have many ways, via email, text messages, online conference calls and other correspondence to follow up and disciple others.

Years ago, I came across Proverb 13:20, which says, "Whoever walks with the wise will become wise." I began to pray that the Lord would open opportunities for me to spend quality time with men and women who have godly wisdom. He has been faithful in answering that prayer over the years. Shortly after, I began praying that prayer, the Lord allowed me to get acquainted with some amazing individuals.

Retired missionaries and authors Bertha Smith and Dr. C. L. Culpepper, who both served as missionaries in China and experienced firsthand the great Shantung Revival of 1927-1937. In addition to hearing Miss Bertha speak on several occasions, my wife, Sheila and I had the privilege of spending three days with her at Peniel Prayer Center in Cowpens, S. C. She taught us the importance of staying current with confessing our sins and what it means to experience the fulness of the Holy Spirit. Miss Bertha was active in ministry and influenced many until she went to be with the Lord at almost 100 years of age.

It was also a joy to sit under the teaching of Dr. C. L. Culpepper while in seminary. What I remember most about Dr. Culpepper was that he almost always lectured in tears. He had such a tender heart toward the Lord, having been deeply impacted by the Shantung Revival and how the Lord worked during that season. He obviously longed for the Lord to move in such a way again in our day and in this country. Like Miss Bertha, he had a great passion for helping others understand the Holy Spirit's work and experience the Spirit-filled life. Hearing and learning how God has moved in great power in the past gives us hope that He can do it again. There are many signs that we could be on the verge of the next spiritual awakening and perhaps a significant accelerating of the spread of the Gospel.

GOD AT WORK THROUGHOUT HISTORY

The more we are aware of the work of God throughout history, the greater our desire and expectation will be to experience and share it with others. An important quote that is worthy of reflecting on is from A. W. Tozer; he said:

- Anything God has ever done at any time, He can do now.
- Anything He has ever done anywhere; He can do here.
- Anything He has ever done through anyone; He can do through you.

The life and ministry of Henry Scougal has been an inspiring story for me and many others who have a heart for the Lord and His will and purpose. Scougal is best known for a small book titled *The Life of God in the Soul of Man*. It originated as a private letter to a friend. Then it was published in book form in 1677. His book was a significant influence on the lives of Charles and John Wesley. Charles gave a copy to George Whitefield. After reading that book, he became convinced that he must be born again and testified that he never knew what true religion was until he read that book. Whitefield later became a catalyst for the first Great Awakening in the seventeen hundreds and greatly impacted the world by advancing the Great Commission.

In 1997 the Lord gave me the privilege of facilitating the founding of the Dunham Bible Museum on the campus of Houston Christian University. For several years I had the opportunity of researching the history of the Bible, as well as the history of printing, Bible translation work, and the history of Spiritual Awakenings. It is inspiring and encouraging to discover how God has used certain individuals that have changed the course of history. It has been a long time since we have experienced a move of God that has changed the culture and structures of society. However, increasing numbers of Church and Mission leaders believe we could very likely be on the verge of a new wave of revival and awakening.

SPARKS THAT IGNITE

Samuel J. Mills, as mentioned earlier, is another example of how one person can influence and have great impact for advancing the Kingdom. As a student at Williams College in Massachusetts in the early 1800s, Mills led what became known as the famous haystack prayer meeting in 1806. He was also a prime mover in founding the first foreign mission societies in North America, in addition to being a catalyst in the Bible Society movement during the Second Great Awakening.

Several local Bible Societies were formed during that period. Mills suggested that there would be a need for a national Bible society as part of the evangelical efforts. He has been recognized as the father of foreign missions in North America. Interestingly, both Scougal and Mills both died as young men. Scougal was only in his late twenties, and Mill was thirty-five when he passed away. These two men are examples of what Robert E. Coleman talks about in his book, *The Spark That Ignites*, which was later republished as *The Coming World Revival.*

God is still at work today, looking for those whose hearts are turned to Him so He can show Himself strong on our behalf, as we read in Scripture. Henry Blackaby and the late Dr. Avery Willis are two men the Lord has used in significant ways over the past few decades. Getting to know them personally and working closely with Avery in the formative days of the International Orality Network was a blessing and a privilege, as he was the first Executive Director. He had previously served as Senior Vice President of the International Mission Board of the Southern Baptist Convention and oversaw the work of more than six thousand missionaries. Dr. Willis, who developed a disciple making program and is author of Master Life, believed that the Orality Movement is one of the most significant breakthroughs in global mission strategies that have taken place over the past five hundred years. He often emphasized that the genius of the movement is that it is a return to the simple methods of the Early Church. It's how Jesus communicated, trained, made disciples and the most effective ways people have learned and communicated from the beginning of time.

EXPERIENCING GOD

Back in the early 1990s, when I first met and heard Henry Blackaby speak, I thought his messages sounded a lot like a couple of others I had known and benefited from their teachings, the late Manley Beasley and Miss Bertha Smith. One day while visiting Henry, I asked about his possible connections with them. He shared that both of them also influenced his life. Manley used to say our main challenge in life is to "find out what God is up to and get in on it." Henry had another way of saying it, "Identify the activity of God, and join Him." The well-known book that he authored, along with Claude King, *Experiencing God,* gives a thorough treatment of these concepts and has had a major impact on perhaps millions of lives since its release. Another great book I recommend is *On Mission with God*, co-authored by Avery Willis and Henry Blackaby.

Since repetition is the mother of all learning (as the saying goes), I like to emphasize that throughout history, God seems to have used common, ordinary people to do extraordinary things. He is still doing so today, which makes each of us candidates for having a significant impact on the Kingdom of God. Many of those who have gained notoriety are often referred to as great men or women of God. I'm reminded of something I've heard Ian Thomas say regarding that. He said there is no such thing as a great man or woman of God. There is just a great God, and He is willing to be as great as He is through any man, woman, boy, or girl who will totally surrender to and make themselves available to Him.

When we think about leadership and influence, it is fascinating to discover those who have influenced the most influential. In many cases a little-known person may have been behind the scenes mentoring or discipling those who become notable and well known. I'm sure we will discover in heaven the many common, ordinary individuals who made a significant contribution to the kingdom of God but were never noticed here on earth.

It was interesting to learn years ago how Billy Graham was influenced by Stephen Olford. Luis Palau was influenced by Ian Thomas. Norman Grubb greatly influenced Abraham Vereide, who was instrumental in the beginning of the National Prayer Breakfast movement. Originally known as the Presidential Prayer Breakfast in the early 1950s, beginning in Washington D. C. and has now spread around the world. Many prominent world leaders, members of Congress, members of Parliament, business leaders, and even heads of state have been impacted, and many have come to Christ through the Prayer Breakfast Movement.

Having spent considerable time in Africa, Asia, and Latin America over the years, it is always interesting and amazing to discover how the Gospel was introduced to those regions. Then consider what it will take to get the Gospel to the unreached, unengaged people groups in our time. Of course, there are still a few hundred Bible-less people groups, the least and last, who still need and have never heard the Good News of Jesus. In addition to those remote, faraway places, most of us rub shoulders with unreached people in our normal traffic patterns. It makes a big difference when we recognize that, as followers of Jesus, we are on mission with God. We literally live in a mission field and can be salt and light every day, wherever we happen to be.

Meet the Author

Jerry Wiles is President Emeritus of Living Water International, serves as Ambassador-at-Large with the International Orality Network, and Mission Advisor with Missio Nexus. He has more than fifty years of experience in ministry and international mission work and has served on the boards of several ministry and mission organizations. His highly effective and innovative communication and disciple making style has been acclaimed by a broad spectrum of church leaders.

He has received worldwide recognition for his outreach strategy development and is recognized as a paradigm pioneer in the Orality Movement. As an author, radio program producer, and conference speaker, he has been a frequent guest on radio and television talk shows and traveled extensively as a public speaker. Jerry is an Air Force veteran, a former business professional, pastor, and university administrator.

You Can Connect with Jerry at:
JerryWiles.com

Printed in the USA
CPSIA information can be obtained
at www.ICGtesting.com
CBHW052024221024
16238CB00016B/1055

9 781951 648848